KU-737-122

821·4
WAL

PARADISE LOST
AND ITS CRITICS

Paradise Lost
AND ITS CRITICS

BY

A. J. A. WALDOCK

R478

STIRLING COUNTY LIBRARY

CAMBRIDGE
AT THE UNIVERSITY PRESS
1961

569393

821.4

WAL

PUBLISHED BY
THE SYNDICS OF THE CAMBRIDGE UNIVERSITY PRESS

Bentley House, 200 Euston Road, London, N.W. 1
American Branch: 32 East 57th Street, New York 22, N.Y.
West African Office: P.O. Box 33, Ibadan, Nigeria

First edition   1947
First paperback edition 1961

Reprinted in the United States of America

CONTENTS

CONTENTS

PREFACE

ONE of the notable events of contemporary criticism has been the rediscovery of *Paradise Lost*: one might almost say the discovery of it, so new have been some of the viewpoints taken, so fresh some of the significances gathered. Any such accumulation of comment brings with it the need, sooner or later, for a scrutiny of its processes, and it is with such a scrutiny that this book is very largely concerned. It is an attempt to assess the validity of some of the most important among recent critical interpretations of the poem.

I naturally make at the same time my own efforts to reach the truth about *Paradise Lost*; and here one deceptively simple question seems recurrent: the question of what, at this important juncture or that, is really *happening* in the poem. It is strange, perhaps, that there should be debate about what goes on—about what really takes place—in a work so clear to all appearance in outline, and of so ringing a definiteness in expression, as *Paradise Lost*. But there is debate. Critics differ not only in their approach to the poem, in their feeling about it, in their judgement of it: they differ also in their understanding of what occurs in it. The question, wherever it appears, is obviously fundamental.

I have to thank my colleagues in the English Department at Sydney University, first and chiefly Mr R. G. Howarth, then Dr A. G. Mitchell and Mr H. J. Oliver, for much helpful advice and comment. I owe a similar debt, despite profound differences of feeling, to my former colleague, Professor I. R. Maxwell, now of Melbourne; and to Professor S. Musgrove, of Auckland University College, I am grateful for the clarification and the stimulus that come from friendly but energetic controversy.

A. J. A. W.

CHAPTER I

THE POET AND THE THEME

THIRTY YEARS or so ago scholars began to ask a new question about *Paradise Lost*. It was a question that in the long history of Milton criticism had never, really, been asked before. It was a question that would have caused Johnson to raise his eyebrows; and not only Johnson; it would have caused Coleridge and Arnold to raise theirs; it would have surprised Raleigh. The question was: what does Milton *mean* in *Paradise Lost*?

This question was really novel. The poem, of course, had always had its problems, but these in the main had been technical. Even the age-long question, Who is the hero? had been, after all, a technical problem, permitted in the end mercifully to lapse, shelved rather than settled, when at last it had become apparent that each of the four or five possible answers was equally right—or wrong—since each was the answer to a separate question. Dryden thought the Devil was Milton's hero, and we must agree that he was, if we are thinking (with Dryden) in terms of a giant who foils the knight and drives him out of his stronghold. Addison felt that if any person in the poem deserved the name it was the Messiah, 'who is the Hero, both in the Principal action, and in the chief Episodes';[1] and in this too there is a rightness. But it is Adam, as Landor pointed out, 'who acts and suffers most, and on whom the consequences have most influence'.[2] Is he not therefore the main character? In a sense, we see clearly, he is. But again, Adam is Man; his fate is that of all his progeny; should not we say, then, that the true hero

1 *Spectator*, No. 297.
2 *Imaginary Conversations* (Southey and Landor, first conversation).

of the poem is the Human Race? In a sense, we must. And when M. Saurat, at the end of all, declares that nothing of this is to the point and produces for us the true hero at last—Milton himself—we must admit that in this assertion too, which triumphantly cuts the knot of the whole difficulty, there is a kind of reason. It seems obvious that each of these solutions is the right one—for a certain problem; each is the correct answer to a question, but the questions are not the same.

Neither this problem, however, nor any other was radical. Blake in his rather unhelpful paradox might suggest the presence of unresolved conflicts in Milton's mind, and in doing so point the way to those theories of our own time that find 'unconscious' meanings in the poem somewhat at odds with Milton's conscious intentions; but I doubt whether before the twentieth century it had ever seriously occurred to a reader of *Paradise Lost* to wonder what Milton was driving at. Some readers, indeed, had appeared to find the drift almost a little too clear for their comfort. 'The underlying thoughts are few,' said Bagehot, 'though the flowers on the surface are so many.'[1] Keats hoped that it would not be presuming, even between friends, to say that Milton's philosophy, human and divine, 'may be tolerably understood by one not much advanced in years'.[2] Plainly the poem had not yet been thought of as in any serious way problematical; it was still felt, and so until recent years continued to be felt, as a poem of quite unmistakable intention, a poem indeed, of rather exceptional clarity of outline, a poem that said what it had to say (even if that was thought by some to be not very much) with superb force and unquestionable point.

We may perhaps take, as representing the best critical opinion at the end of the nineteenth century, Raleigh's witty, suave and penetrating survey. There are no mysteries in

1 *Literary Studies*, ed. R. H. Hutton (1859), vol. I, p. 205.
2 *Letters*, ed. Maurice Buxton Forman (1935), p. 144.

Paradise Lost for Raleigh. He sees, of course, or thinks he sees, all that by the limitations of the theme or by Milton's own limitations of vision is ruled out, all that we must not fairly look for here. Subtle notations of emotion, sudden 'fidelities' to the mixed texture of human experience: these in the main were beside Milton's purpose, as perhaps in any case, Raleigh thinks, beyond his powers. Eve's quick spasm of jealousy at the thought of a successor and supplanter he considers to be about as near an approach to drama in the handling of a human situation as is to be found in all *Paradise Lost*. Indeed it was necessary in such a work to keep humanity at arm's length, to insulate the poem from contact with customary life, and shield it from everyday intimacies of feeling. 'The introduction, in *Paradise Lost*, of a real human child, such as Shakespeare brings into *Coriolanus* or *Macbeth*, would be like the bringing of a spark of fire into a powder magazine.'[1] Raleigh feels nothing more acutely than this carefully preserved isolation, the 'artificial perspectives' that Milton is obliged to maintain to keep the system of his poem intact. Such a work could at no time, 'not even in the most theological of ages', have borne the more searching tests of realism and verisimilitude; all the more wonderful, Raleigh thinks, is the art by which this 'gigantic filamented structure' has been raised into the air. There it stands like some enchanted palace, a monument to the miraculous skill of its maker—just stands, and no more: 'but that it should stand at all is the marvel, seeing that it is spanned on frail arches over the abyss of the impossible, the unnatural, and the grotesque'.[2] It is the precariousness of the achievement that Raleigh intensely feels, the quality of *Paradise Lost* as a sheer feat, a majestic *tour de force*. Taking his 'wildly intractable'[3] material (so Raleigh sees it) Milton reared a structure that by all the laws of poetic engineering should collapse under

1 *Milton* (1900), p. 122.   2 Op. cit. pp. 123–4

3 Ibid. p. 255.

its own incredible stresses; wonderfully it holds, poised in its perilous equilibrium, an edifice within which one hardly dares whisper for fear of bringing the whole fabric crashing down. *Paradise Lost* does not *say* much to Raleigh, does not speak strongly to his heart. But he recognizes the 'power', the 'vagueness', and the 'grandeur', and can yield himself imaginatively to those. Above all he sees in the work a sublime triumph of craftsmanship, an achievement in which problems that one would have deemed beyond all human solution are yet somehow victoriously solved. Raleigh feels that on the whole they *are* solved, that the superhuman elevation is maintained, that the 'preternaturally majestic diction' accomplishes its object, that the structure, despite the unbelievable stresses, is firm; and he stands back from it and gazes at it with admiration and astonishment and awe.

It is in the second decade, I think, after Raleigh wrote that one begins to notice the first definite signs of a change of attitude. There was now a stirring in Milton criticism. What had absorbed Raleigh was Milton's technical conquest of his problems; it had never struck Raleigh that there could be serious doubt about what Milton was trying to do. But now this question itself is raised. The poem, so transparent (it had always seemed) in aim, now takes on a certain cloudiness; patches in it begin to blur.

In 1917, for example, the late Edwin Greenlaw contributed to *Studies in Philology* an article entitled 'A Better Teacher than Aquinas'. Greenlaw's chief purpose was to investigate the influence of Spenser on Milton. Dryden had declared categorically in the Preface to his *Fables*: 'Milton has acknowledg'd to me that Spenser was his original.' We have, as well, Milton's own testimony at the end of the famous passage in the *Areopagitica* in which he has spoken of the nature of true virtue and how it must stand its test in the world as it is: 'which was the reason why our sage and serious Poet Spenser, whom I dare be known to think a better teacher than Scotus or Aquinas, describing true temperance under the person of Guion, brings him in with his palmer through the cave of Mammon and the bowr of earthly blisse, that he might see and know, and yet abstain.' Greenlaw explores the full significance of these declarations, comparing the book of Guyon with analogous parts of *Paradise Lost*, and reaches the conclusion that Milton is indebted to Spenser for not much less than the central theme of his poem. For, as Greenlaw sees it, the theme of *Paradise Lost* is not quite what Milton said it was—Man's first disobedience and the Fall—or at least is not to be taken as limited by the terms of this opening definition. Underneath is a conception that gives this announced theme its real meaning and point: the conflict in man's soul between the principles of reason and unreason. The struggle itself is exemplified in what Greenlaw feels to be the two interlocking 'adventures' of *Paradise Lost*, the story of Satan and the story of the temptation and fall of Adam. Satan is shown as mastered by one type of intemperance—'unworthy ambition and lust for power'; Adam by another—sensuality. 'The dominating theme of the entire story' is temperance. Thus, Greenlaw insists, the philosophy of *Paradise Lost* is ultimately from Greece, not Genesis. 'Adam fell because the irrational element in his soul, inflamed by a provoking object, triumphed over temperance, not because he disobeyed [as Raleigh had expressed it] a whimsical Tyrant, all of whose laws are arbitrary and occasional, and who exacts from his creatures an obedience that differs from brute submission in one point only, that by the gift of free-will it is put within their power to disobey.'[1] And again, summing up the whole: 'The story of the fall of Adam immediately gains significance and interest if we recognize that the apple is but a symbol, and that Milton's real theme is to show how Adam fell because he did not stand the test of temperance.'[2]

1 *Studies in Philology* (April 1917), vol. XIV, p. 201.
2 Ibid. p. 213.

I will not stay at this point to comment on Greenlaw's Spenserian thesis. I do not think it can be doubted that he drives his analogies very hard. He finds them in other books of the *Faerie Queene* as well. After the Fall and the quarrel between Adam and Eve 'the analogy between the story of Adam and that of Redcrosse becomes very marked', and Greenlaw traces it point by point. Redcrosse is led astray by Duessa and falls into the hands of Orgoglio; Despair tries to induce him to kill himself; Una saves him; and then, with the arrival of Arthur, comes 'a period of purgation and training in preparation for salvation'—the sojourn in the house of Cœlia. 'All these steps', Greenlaw thinks, 'are followed by Milton.'[1] This, surely, is nonsense.

The real interest of Greenlaw's article lies in the view that it expresses of the nature of *Paradise Lost*. I make one or two remarks on this and on the general attitude to the poem that the article discloses.

One sentence seems to me particularly noteworthy—I have already quoted it: 'The story of the fall of Adam immediately gains significance and interest if we recognize that the apple is but a symbol, and that Milton's real theme is to show how Adam fell because he did not stand the test of temperance.' 'The real theme': it was a new phrase in serious and reasoned discussion of *Paradise Lost*, a phrase that would have sounded oddly in the ears of the Milton critics of previous centuries. It is interesting to remember what Addison made of the 'real theme', or, as he called it, the 'great Moral' of the poem, a moral, he thought, 'the most universal and most useful that can be imagined'. It was this: 'that Obedience to the Will of God makes men happy, and that Disobedience makes them miserable.' Here, said Addison, 'is visibly the Moral of the principal Fable which turns upon Adam and Eve, who continued in Paradise while they kept the Command that was given them, and were driven out of it as soon as they had

1 Loc. cit. p. 214

transgressed.'[1] This, we may say, was very unsophisticated, and we may agree readily enough that the possibilities of meaning—indeed, the patent meanings—in *Paradise Lost* are hardly exhausted by Addison's summary of its scope. And yet, when Addison tells us that the *visible* moral of the principal Fable is just what he proceeds to assert, it is not very easy, surely, to contradict him. The opposition between Reason and Passion, we know well, is deeply embedded in the theory of *Paradise Lost*. The idea of 'temperance' is there too, and perhaps in certain passages seems to us to be not far distant from the heart of the poem. Yet in the complex and difficult business of assessing a literary masterpiece nothing, I suppose, is of much greater importance than that we should make a determined effort to put first things first, and to keep second things second. The 'visible' moral of the poem—the moral that is proclaimed at the outset, that is dwelt on and driven home at innumerable points throughout it, that is stated and reiterated by God, man, angels and the Devil himself—is the moral that Addison enunciates. And we may wonder whether Greenlaw, in making all turn on the Platonic virtue of temperance and ranking everything else in the poem as subordinate to this prime meaning, has not, after all, succeeded in elevating what is properly a second thing into the place of a first.

There is something else deserving note in the sentence quoted. 'The story of the fall of Adam immediately gains significance and interest if we recognize....' There are tell-tale signs here I think, of the attitude (largely, no doubt, unconscious) that is behind the article. Greenlaw, in a sense, is rescuing *Paradise Lost*. Earlier in the article he had pointed out the curious parallelism between the destiny of Milton's great poem and the destiny of Spenser's in critical history. 'Both great poems have been patronized for their insufficiency of thought; Spenser's poem has been criticized for

[1] *Spectator*, No. 369.

vagueness, lack of structure, tedious length, and because it is an "allegory"; Milton's for inconsistency, for representing an outworn theology, and for triviality. Both poets have been praised chiefly for certain "poetic" qualities at the expense of intellectual power, a judgement which they would have resented.'[1] Greenlaw resents it too. He sees, at any rate, the implication that lies dormant in such praise and such blame; it would be hard, if such praise and blame were true, to predict for *Paradise Lost* any lasting future except as a majestic derelict, a great white elephant of poetry without real use or function. Even in Raleigh's criticism, intensely appreciative as in so many ways it is, there is perhaps the faint foreshadowing of such a thought. It is clear, at least, that if Raleigh's *Paradise Lost* is the real *Paradise Lost*, the modern mind is out of touch with it; the poem, as interpreted by Raleigh, has no real chance of speaking to the modern mind, any more than it spoke to Raleigh's mind. And yet it would be a pity if this were so: that is what Greenlaw feels. It would be a good thing for us and for *Paradise Lost* if beneath the announced theme and its 'triviality' it were possible to find another and better one, hitherto missed—a 'real theme' —of richer significance, and wider appeal. I think we may see in Greenlaw's article the first of a number of attempts to refit *Paradise Lost* for the modern mind.

Greenlaw and his fellow American scholars, in conjunction with a less numerous European group, began a movement that by 1920 or so had developed a picture of Milton as thinker and poet that differed in many important respects from the traditional image. Essentially he was regarded now as a Renaissance artist and no longer in any narrow or painful or disturbing way as a Puritan. The work of M. Saurat, as he himself says, lay a little outside that of both these groups, though he was extremely sympathetic towards their results. What was felt a little curious was that no English scholar

1 Loc. cit. p. 201.

had joined the movement. Professor Grierson, indeed, showed great interest in what was going on, intervening often to correct an excess or to redress a balance that, as it seemed to him, had been upset. Now he will hint to Liljegren that English scholars do not, after all, cling quite as tightly as some Continental critics think to the austere, unmodified Puritan tradition of Milton. Now he will interpose to suggest that Saurat is pressing the results of his researches a little hard, and that Christian doctrine in Milton's thought is, after all, still basic. At another time he will turn aside to reprove gently a French scholar who at this late day has misguidedly written a paper on *Adam est-il le héros du poème?* It is a question, Grierson tells him, that 'we in this country have long ago settled'.[1] Grierson in this way observed, supervised and corrected; but not yet had England produced a New Miltonian. England produced one (though with a difference) in 1930.

The critical attitude embodied in Dr Tillyard's *Milton* is of such interest that I must pause for a brief note on it.

I will begin with two quotations. This is the first paragraph of Dr Tillyard's Introduction:

No one reading through *Paradise Lost* with any degree of seriousness can help asking with what the poem as a whole is most truly concerned, what were the feelings and ideas that dominated Milton's mind when he wrote it. Such was my own experience, and when I found the question difficult to answer, I sought help from the books on Milton that are most read in England. But they helped very little. The majority, however good on other topics, made no attempt at all to answer this particular question; or what they did say went no further than to summarize Milton's own professions as to the true subject of his poem. The only critics who seemed to tackle the problem in the right kind of way were the Satanists, namely those who invested the character of Satan with all that Milton felt and valued most strongly. But the more I considered the Satanic explanation, the more inadequate it seemed: far too simple to solve so complicated a problem. And so I was led to work out my own solution, the results of which attempt are the central part of this book. I found

---

1 *The Year's Work in English Studies*, 1920–1, p. 104; 1927, p. 204; 1928, p. 202.

in due course that more had been written on the subject than I had known, especially in America, where opinion had already reacted against the Satanists; but nothing I have read has convinced me that there is not room for several more attempts to find out with what *Paradise Lost* as a whole is most truly concerned.

And this is the first paragraph of his section on *Paradise Lost*:

> It is strange how little, till quite recently, critics have concerned themselves with the meaning of *Paradise Lost*. The style, the versification, the celestial geography, the thought, who is the hero: all these have concerned the critics far more than what the poem is really about, the true state of Milton's mind when he wrote it. Perhaps to those of earlier generations the meaning appeared too simple to need discussion: does not Milton himself tell us all we need to know about it in his opening lines? But such simple-mindedness can ill satisfy a generation which is sceptical of professed motives and which suspects the presence of others, either concealed or not realized by the author. It is not surprising, then, that in the last ten years or so there has been more discussion of the subject than in all the rest of the time during which *Paradise Lost* has been in print. From the differences of opinion it may be judged that the question has by no means been settled, and another attempt to answer it may well be pardoned.

It is perhaps not quite fair to isolate these passages. It is certain that we may object to every one of the literary principles they proclaim and yet be grateful for the study to which these principles led. Dr Tillyard's work has enlarged our knowledge of Milton on every side. Nevertheless, it would be difficult, I think, to find elsewhere in Milton criticism so compact a cluster of questionable assumptions. Observe, first, how Greenlaw's conception of a 'real theme' returns, but now with an interesting difference. Greenlaw in the course of his investigations lighted on what seemed to him the real theme of *Paradise Lost*, and was very pleased to find it; but he does not impress one as having always known it was there. Dr Tillyard, before he begins his investigations, *knows* that there is a deeper meaning in *Paradise Lost* than the meaning that is obvious: this is not something that has to be demonstrated: it is self-evident. What *Paradise Lost* seems to be about, or even what Milton tells us it is about, cannot be what it is really about: Dr Tillyard takes this for granted. I do not think that anything he goes on to say in the paragraphs in question can alter the flatness of this initial assumption: the flatness of it would, I think, have left the Milton critics of every previous age somewhat astonished.

But what Dr Tillyard goes on to say is equally interesting. He gives us, for example, some hint of what he has in mind by the 'real meaning' of *Paradise Lost* when he refers to 'the feelings and ideas that dominated Milton's mind' when he wrote it. If we can reach these feelings and ideas we shall be in a much stronger position, he considers, to judge of the true theme of the poem. He goes further: the state of Milton's mind when he wrote the poem *is* the theme: this, if we can find it, is 'what the poem is really about'.

Such a statement of the problem of *Paradise Lost* was not allowed to go unchallenged. Mr C. S. Lewis took up Dr Tillyard's words and objected to the 'concealed major premiss' in them—that all poetry is *about* the poet's state of mind. Dr Tillyard in due course replied, and the result was their engaging controversy, *The Personal Heresy* (1939). The controversy ranged very widely, returning only at infrequent intervals to its starting-point in Dr Tillyard's remarks on the 'true meaning' of *Paradise Lost*, and I have no intention, beyond a bare word, of intruding into it. On the whole the issues raised, complex and subtle as they were, seem to me to have no very direct bearing on the problems of *Paradise Lost*. Once or twice, however, the argumentation in its wheelings made contact with the special question of the narrative poem as such, and some points then emerged that are of real importance for this discussion.

Mr Lewis early in the debate—indeed at the very opening of it—had remarked that drama and epic, on the face of them, seemed to give very ready support to the 'impersonal theory of poetry' that he was advocating. Dr Tillyard touched on this matter when it came up again at a later stage, but dealt with it in a way that (to me, at least) seems to show a distinct weakening of his position. After saying that he yields nothing to Mr Lewis in enjoyment of narrative verse he proceeds: 'But I am far from certain that even a narrative poem is about the story it narrates, in the sense of the story being the poem's end. We do not doubt that Vasco da Gama sailed round the Cape to India or that Camoens wrote an epic on that subject. And as a matter of policy it was expedient that Camoens should write under the impression that his first job was to tell a story. To have had qualms about the solidity of the story, to know that it was in danger of evaporating would have been fatal to the kind of concentration necessary to poetic composition.'[1] And Dr Tillyard makes the point that a writer of fiction, of whatever kind it may be, must certainly have imaginative faith in his story while he is writing it, if he is to write it well. But the question of the real 'end'—or, if we like, the real meaning—of Camoens's epic remains. 'What kind of existence the voyage of Da Gama has when told by Camoens is far too abstruse a question for me to answer. But I feel fairly confident that for a rough description of Camoens's real, though unadmitted, ends in the poem the phrase, "What it felt like to be alive in Portugal and its empire about the middle of the sixteenth century", would be far closer the truth than "Vasco da Gama's voyage to India".'[2] This, then, is what Camoens's poem is 'most truly' about. It will be observed that Dr Tillyard does not go so far as to say that it is about 'the true state of Camoens's mind when he wrote it'—only that it is about an external something a little different from the external something that its title might superficially suggest, or from what Camoens, if pressed, might himself have described as its subject. But 'what it felt like to be alive in Portugal' and so on is a thoroughly objective

1 Op. cit. p. 134.   2 Ibid. p. 135.

theme: Dr Tillyard is substituting one objective theme for another, that is all; by this instance, at all events, he is not showing in the slightest degree that what a poem is most truly concerned with is the state of mind of its author.

As further proof of his contention that poets do not really tell stories at all (the notion that they do, he thinks, 'is a fiction') he points to the extraordinary differences that we may observe between several poetic versions of the same subject-matter: between the fall of Troy, say, as treated in *The Trojan Women* and the same topic as treated in the second book of *The Aeneid*. Such differences certainly exist and may be very remarkable; but is it really true to say that they 'make us doubt the solidity of the stories themselves'? They make us doubt, perhaps, the existence of an authentic proto-type in the background—of a master-story, say, of Troy, to which all other stories of Troy are referable. But if we come to feel that these type-stories in themselves have no very definite outline, but rather a wavery existence, is that of very much consequence? A horse in the abstract is perhaps but a figment: does that matter in practice, as long as there are horses? Dr Tillyard seems to be thinking of an ideal entity—in this case the story of Troy—which becomes less distinct and 'real' with each successive variation upon it. But if each variation itself is distinct and real, what of it? It is true of course that if the type-story is well known and if the variations upon it are too wide, we are likely to be disconcerted; but that is hardly the point here. There is no reason, surely, why there should not be a dozen stories of Tristram or of Cressid all equally solid. They will, of course, be different stories, not the same story at all; but that will not affect their reality, or mean that we must give up examining 'apparent subject-matter' and apply ourselves, instead, to examining 'states of mind'. There is a play *King Lear* and a 'true chronicle history of King Leir', and numerous other stories of Lear besides. But what the 'real' story of

Lear is who could say, or what meaning could there be in
such a question? The story exists in its versions and can exist,
surely, in no other way.

We may make the application to *Paradise Lost*. It is certain
that everything that we can find out about Milton's mind
while he was writing the poem, or about his mind before
he began to write it, will be of help to us in the understanding of the poem itself. Perhaps he himself changed
somewhat during the years in which he was composing it;
if he did, and if we can be sure what the changes were, we
shall have again a means of illumination. All this we understand; and one of the great values of Dr Tillyard's book lies
precisely in its careful plotting of the whole course of Milton's
development from 'origins' to the last line of his last poem.
But to say that 'what the poem is really about' is 'the true
state of Milton's mind when he wrote it' seems a mere confusion. Nor is it (as we have seen) a slip of the pen. Dr Tillyard
seems to mean what he says. 'The meaning of a poem is not
the story told, the statements made, the philosophy stated,
but the state of mind, valuable or otherwise, revealed by the
sum of all the elements of the poem.' If that is true we can
only feel that chaos is come again, for it almost removes the
possibility of our ever coming to grips with a work of literature. How much, after all, do we know or *can* we know about
the true state of Shakespeare's mind when he was writing
King Lear? How much does it concern us to know about it?
We have *King Lear*, and the sum of all the elements of *King
Lear* is still—*King Lear*. Can we properly think of a work of
literature as if it were connected by a kind of umbilical cord
with its maker—as if its maker were still pumping life into
it? *Paradise Lost* (like *Lear*) is there, apart from its creator,
'on its own'. Not quite so definitely, perhaps, 'on its own'
as *Lear* is, for we know very well that Milton's private moods
have, in fact, marked the poem; here and there, in this passage
or that, we are conscious—too conscious, sometimes—of what

Milton's 'true state of mind' was as he wrote. But the effect of such passages, in general, is rather to distort the meaning than to reinforce it. In the same way, if his spirit and outlook really did alter during the writing the result could well be (it would not necessarily be) some lack of harmony between the several parts. Nothing of this, and no distinctions that we may draw between the mind of Milton as man, and the mind of Milton as poet, can, it seems to me, make much difference to the obstinate fact that *Paradise Lost* is an epic poem of singularly hard and definite outline, expressing itself (or so at least would be our first impressions) with unmistakable clarity and point. One agrees very readily with Dr Tillyard that the sound of the words contributes to the meaning, is indeed a part of it, and (a point that he well makes) that the construction is a part of it too. Everything in or of the poem is part of its meaning. But the distinction between what an author feels and what he does, between what goes on in his mind as he writes and what he writes, must surely remain.

One further point in Dr Tillyard's programme is noteworthy. Earlier generations, he remarks, perhaps found Milton's meaning too plain to need much discussion. 'But such simple-mindedness can ill satisfy a generation which is sceptical of professed motives and which suspects the presence of others, either concealed or not realized by the author.' Dr Tillyard gives much attention to these unrealized motives or 'unconscious meanings'. I reserve till a later chapter some discussion of his findings.

And I will not make any attempt at this point to trace in further detail the progress of Milton criticism in the twentieth century. I suppose no short study of *Paradise Lost* has commanded more attention than the late Mr Charles Williams's brief introduction to the new 'World's Classics' edition of the *English Poems* (1940). It was an introduction that to one reader, at least, signalized nothing less than 'the recovery of a true critical tradition after more than a hundred years of laborious misunderstanding'. That was no small thing to say. It was said by Mr C. S. Lewis in dedicating to Mr Williams his own book, *A Preface to Paradise Lost* (1942). And with a brief preparatory note on this—undoubtedly one of the most provocative and stimulating of all recent studies of the poem—I may conclude this short preliminary survey.

Mr Lewis's approach is interestingly different from Dr Tillyard's. Dr Tillyard, as we have seen, set out to find *Paradise Lost*. Mr Lewis has no need to undertake this quest. He has already found the poem; his aim is rather to explain it. The keynote of his book is struck in the opening sentence: 'The first qualification for judging any piece of workmanship from a corkscrew to a cathedral is to know *what* it is—what it was intended to do and how it is meant to be used.' Mr Lewis's grand object, therefore, is to show what Milton meant his poem to be. Thus, of the style: it has been blamed for being ritualistic, incantatory and artificial; Mr Lewis's answer is that Milton intended it to be all those things, for only by the method of ritual could Milton have accomplished his aims. He explains, again, how the hierarchical conception penetrates *Paradise Lost*. It is a conception that has become a little unfamiliar to us; we must therefore make some effort to grasp it if we would understand Milton's purposes aright. Once more, of Adam and Eve: Mr Lewis tells us that in earlier years he had misunderstood Milton's drift. He had come to the poem 'associating innocence with childishness', and that was why Raleigh's remark, 'Adam from the depth of his inexperience is lavishly sententious', had amused him, and had seemed to him to put neatly a real defect in Milton's picture of our first parents. But now, as he explains, he sees that Adam was never truly 'inexperienced', was never (though innocent) childish, was never intended by Milton to make on us an impression of naïve, unsophisticated, primitive man. Mr Lewis's exposition is delightfully conducted; and it may be doubted whether any other critic has made so resolute an attempt to take *Paradise Lost* from beginning to end on Milton's own terms. In his final chapter he sums up and weighs the valid objections, of which, in his opinion, there are only two that we need take very seriously into account. The poem, with its 'untransmuted lump of futurity' in the two last books, suffers from a grave structural flaw; and the presentation of God is open to some criticism. These, he considers, are the major reservations that we must make in our estimate—indeed the only reservations that we need actually make at all. When they have been made, Mr Lewis thinks, 'the case of the *advocatus diaboli* against *Paradise Lost* is complete'. Everything else is on the credit side. Even the theme, as treated by Milton, 'fulfils the conditions of great story better perhaps than any other, for, more than any other, it leaves things where it did not find them'.[1]

It seems almost too easy; and I think it is too easy. We may admit, certainly, that it is of the highest importance that we should be conversant with Milton's presuppositions —should have learnt the rules of his game. Mr Lewis himself helps notably to elucidate these rules for us. But with the learning of them, he almost suggests, the task is finished. 'Only grasp what Milton is driving at', he seems to say, 'and the battle is over; only understand what Milton *meant* and you will see that there are no real difficulties at all.' I do not think even Mr Lewis can persuade us that the case is quite so simple as this.

But it is time to come to details, and I will pause merely for two brief observations on the general problem.

It is possible, I think, to overrate very much Milton's *awareness* of the peculiar difficulties of his theme. The difficulties are of the kind that fairly leap to our eyes. That is partly because, owing to certain types of literary development during the last two centuries or so, we have received an intensive training in the business of estimating the sort of

1 Op. cit. p. 129.

literary problem that is radical in *Paradise Lost*. We have acquired, in plain fact—through the novel, and in other ways —certain types of literary experience that Milton was without. It is not absurd to mention the novel in connection with *Paradise Lost*, for the problems of such a poem and the characteristic problems of the novel have elements in common. The novel has given us an enormous store of precedents. Largely as a result of its history we have built up a technique for assessing at once the practicability of certain themes for literary treatment, a technique that it is not ridiculous to suggest that Milton did not possess in quite the same sense. We have only to look at the material that he was bent on disposing in his epic to see that some of the problems he faced were virtually insoluble. A glance at the story of the Fall as it is given in Genesis shows that it is lined with difficulties of the gravest order. God, to begin with, does not show to advantage in that particular story: the story is a bad one for God. Within that set of events to make God attractive to our common human sensibilities (and it is not to be forgotten that the *raison d'être* of the whole poem lies in its appeal to common human sensibilities) will be hard. Again, it will be necessary to mark the transition from innocence to guilt; somehow sinlessness has to give place to sin; and in a large narrative such a transition may not be easy to make plausible. There is, once more, the disproportion (cruel at least on the face of it) between the offence and the punishment—bringing us back again to God. That apparent disproportion may not trouble us in the biblical story, the miniature; but what of it when the story is magnified a hundred times? Looking back at *Paradise Lost* from what in some real senses is our vantage-point and bringing to bear on it, quite frankly, the whole weight of our own literary experience, we almost catch our breath at the manifold drawbacks of the fable. Could any writer with an instinct for narrative, we ask ourselves, have failed to see what problems those first three chapters of

Genesis held, and to shrink back deterred? At half-a-dozen points difficulties lay in wait that at the slightest prompting might become acute; in any large treatment of the story some of them would necessarily become acute. The story in Genesis was like a stretch of film minutely flawed. Milton's plan was to take this and project it on an enormous canvas. Must he not (we wonder sometimes) have foreseen the effect of the tremendous enlargement: that every slight imperfection would show, that every rift would become a gulf?

He foresaw, it is obvious, nothing of the kind, and one reason, I would suggest, is that he had not the technique for assessing such complications that we (quite involuntarily) possess. The classical epic, it is true, was behind him, but that was not enough. There were no precedents for what he was about to try; so deceptive and difficult a theme on so grandiose a scale *was* something unattempted yet in prose or rhyme.

But there was another reason why he did not detect the problems in his basic fable: he could not, because that fable was God's own truth. We have been taught by M. Saurat and others to recognize the veins of originality in Milton's thinking; his theology was in certain directions adventurous, he was capable of bold and startling speculations. But nothing of this alters appreciably the fact that the Bible for Milton was a document of quite special importance with a place apart and a status of its own. No one reading the patient, painstaking, dogged pages of the *De Doctrina Christiana* can doubt this for a moment. The errors in the transmission of the texts, the chances and changes of their 'uncertain and variable guardianship', only made the task of interpretation the more exciting. But such a task did not mean for Milton the sifting of scriptural truth into different kinds or its assignment to a number of levels. The 'figurativeness' itself (which he concedes) is a figurativeness of strictly limited application, a figurativeness, so to say, that is rather God's concern than ours. God 'accommodates' his account of himself—his feelings, motives and deeds—to the reach of our lowly intelligences. In a sense, then, the account is figurative, but not in any sense that gives us licence to take it lightly. On the contrary, the figurative representations of Scripture are *true*—true for us—in somewhat the same fashion (perhaps we may say) as a physicist's picture-diagram of the atom, if it works, is true for him. Whether the atom is really like that he does not know and perhaps cannot know; all he knows is that it is really like that *for him*. So God gives diagrams of himself which we must accept, for whether they constitute his truth or not they are certainly meant to constitute ours. But the point is plain and I need not insist on it. If Milton felt that the story of the Fall of Man was 'allegorical' that is only to say that he recognized that it might have the symbolism of any other real historical occurrence—might be (in M. Saurat's phrase) 'an allegory of God'. And with an allegory of God what could be wrong?

Here is one of the great paradoxes of *Paradise Lost*. We know that Milton came to his theme gradually and steadily, drawn to it by the deep needs of his nature. Only the highest would suffice him, and of all 'arguments' this was the highest he knew. His choice, then, of form and theme conjoined was in one sense an act of majestic daring. 'He would not take any risk', writes the late Professor Elton, 'short of the heaviest.' And yet in another sense there was *no* risk, provided only he did his own part well, for what theme could be more fully guaranteed, what theme could possibly be safer, than this? It is hardly a wonder if he embarked on it, though with self-searching and awe, yet without excessive anxiety or trepidation. We ponder, as I say, its many disadvantages and are amazed that he himself could ever have overlooked them; must he not have guessed, even if dimly, how in the enormous magnification he intended every tiny rift in the original story would show? The answer of course is that for him there were no rifts; it was out of the question for Milton to admit to himself difficulties in the scriptural story of the Fall—impossible for him, really, to see them. As his work progressed it is clear that he came on problems that he had not expected to encounter. It is of great interest in reading *Paradise Lost* to note that here, or here, a sudden difficulty has checked Milton slightly—that here, or here, a faint uneasiness shows itself. And yet we may take it for granted, I suppose, that Milton never to the end became aware of the real nature of the gravest of the narrative problems he had been grappling with. Just as he began with what must have seemed to him the perfect story, with nothing really that *could* be wrong with it, so at the end, having done his work faithfully and well, it was natural that he should feel that his poem stood four-square, firm-based, an unassailable imaginative whole.

But again: just as Milton could hardly help misconceiving, in certain respects, the imaginative qualities of his chosen theme, so he could hardly help misconceiving, in certain respects, his own relationship to this theme. He believed in it much less intensely than he thought he did.

The point may be illustrated quite easily from the *De Doctrina*, a curiously human document, for all its tessellating laboriousness, and at bottom a very humble work. Essentially, as we know, it is a long fatiguing effort to reconcile the written law with the law of the heart, to bring theology into line with reason—one could almost say to square doctrine with common sense. And it has emotional fluctuations that are extremely interesting. Milton often feels that he is fully succeeding in his self-imposed task. No one can read the chapter 'De Filio' without being sensible of the deep satisfaction with which Milton argues his case. Here, he plainly feels, he *has* brought common sense out triumphant. His feet are on firm ground, he argues with his full mind, sure of his reasoning, interested and eager. Read, again, the pages on predestination, a doctrine which Milton, with the best will in the world, finds himself unable to reconcile (in its rigid form) either with God's fair play or with the innate dignity and freedom of men: the writing has the same confidence and certainty. But now read this:

This sin originated, first, in the instigation of the devil, as is clear from the narrative in Gen. iii. and from 1 John iii. 8, 'he that committeth sin is of the devil, for the devil sinneth from the beginning'. Secondly, in the liability to fall with which man was created, whereby he, as the devil had done before him, 'abode not in the truth', John viii. 44, nor 'kept his first estate, but left his own habitation', Jude 6. If the circumstances of this crime are duly considered, it will be acknowledged to have been a most heinous offence, and a transgression of the whole law. For what sin can be named, which was not included in this one act? It comprehended at once distrust in the divine veracity, and a proportionate credulity in the assurances of Satan; unbelief; ingratitude; disobedience; gluttony; in the man excessive uxoriousness, in the woman a want of proper regard for her husband, in both an insensibility to the welfare of their offspring, and that offspring the whole human race; parricide, theft, invasion of the rights of others, sacrilege, deceit, presumption in aspiring to divine attributes, fraud in the means employed to attain the object, pride and arrogance.[1]

We cannot say that Milton did not believe what he was writing when he penned this account of the multitudinous guilt of our first parents; we can only say that he most definitely did not believe in it in the way in which he believed in the inferiority of the Son (for that doctrine made strong sense to him) or in which he believed in the freedom of man and his responsibility of choice (for those convictions were part of his life).

Nor did he believe, in that way, in the primal happiness. What, after all, has Milton—the Milton of the great famous sayings in the prose works, the Milton who could not praise a fugitive and cloistered virtue unexercised and unbreathed —to do with the effortless innocence, the 'blank' virtue, of prelapsarian man? It is another of the paradoxes of the poem. In many senses *Paradise Lost* was his predestined

1 Book i, chap. x (Columbia, vol. xv, pp. 181–3).

theme, and yet in a sense it put him in a false position, cut clean against the grain of his nature. Believing rather more intensely than the average man that our dignity consists in independent and strenuous thought, and feeling with the same rather exceptional intensity that the essence of life is struggle, he must deplore the coming of thought into the world (for that is what it really amounts to) and represent man's best state as that original featureless blessedness. He was trapped, in a sense, by his theme, and from the trap there was no escape. It is true, as Mr Basil Willey has pointed out,[1] that he bends the myth slightly this way and that, rejecting for example, the 'magic sciential apple' which itself confers knowledge and substituting a taboo. 'It was necessary', he wrote in the *Christian Doctrine*, 'that something should be forbidden or commanded as a test of fidelity, and that an act in its own nature indifferent, in order that man's obedience might be thereby manifested.'[2] Again, with all his regard for learning, certain types of inquiry, as we know, were suspect for Milton, or had become so: these he has no hesitation in associating with the Fall. Raphael says:

> Sollicit not thy thoughts with matters hid; (VIII, 167)

and Adam is adjured to keep to knowledge within bounds. Milton's feelings, no doubt, went with these cautions. In such ways he is able to adapt the story very slightly to his purposes, to win a little freedom and make a private point or two. But there is not, after all, very much that he can do. He can read the myth (or make a valiant attempt to do so) in terms of Passion and Reason, the twin principles of his own humanistic thinking; but with all that, the myth obstinately remains, drawing him away from what most deeply absorbs him (effort, combat, the life of the 'way-faring Christian') to the celebration of a state of affairs that

1 *The Seventeenth Century Background* (1934), pp. 249, 250, 261.
2 Book I, chap. x (Columbia, vol. xv, p. 113).

could never have profoundly interested him, and that he never persuades us does.

An immediate consequence could have been predicted. In a sense Milton's central theme denied him the full expression of his deepest interests. It was likely, then, that as his really deep interests could not find outlet in his poem in the right way they might find outlet in the wrong way. And to a certain extent they do; they find vents and safety-valves often in inopportune places. Adam cannot give Milton much scope to express what he really feels about life: but Satan is there, Satan gives him scope. And the result is that the balance is somewhat disturbed; pressures are set up that are at times disquieting, that seem to threaten more than once, indeed, the equilibrium of the poem.

In approaching the Fall in *Paradise Lost*—or indeed in approaching any part of *Paradise Lost*—there is a simple distinction that it is of the utmost importance, I think, to keep well before the mind. It is this: in reading *Paradise Lost* we must not always expect to find that Milton's intention is perfectly matched by his performance—that what he meant to do in any given case has always its exact counterpart in what he did. Similarly (it is another aspect of the same principle) we must not always expect to find that what he has done is perfectly matched by his *theory* of what he has done; it is quite possible that the view he wishes us to take of a certain matter—the view, perhaps, that he himself, because of the prescriptions of his theme, is compelled to take—may not be in exact accord with the matter as he has actually presented it. Such inconsistencies, if we find them, should not, surely, cause us very much astonishment. Milton was bound as he went on to discover the rigidities and awkwardnesses of his subject; it seems evident that some of them came as a surprise to him, taking him off his guard. The subject, as already suggested, held traps and pitfalls that Milton, for various reasons easy to understand, could not really have foreseen; it was only to be expected that from time to time he would come to the edge of one of these, and, seeing it, would veer sharply away. The traces of such veerings are, I think, perceptible in the poem. Again, in *Paradise Lost* Milton often betrays 'passion' (in very much his own sense of the term). Old emotions surge up and lend a force and fire, or give a pungency, that is not calculated; but the marks that these emotions leave on the writing—the slight distortions to which they give rise—will all be duly recorded in our impressions. If we are ever to see the poem as it really is, our *impressions*, surely, are what we must first and last attend to. Taken as frankly and naturally as we can take them and checked with all possible care, they constitute the facts of the poem. *Paradise Lost* on the face of it is a simple work, and between the impressions of different readers there would under ideal conditions, perhaps, be no great variation. Between the impressions of natural, easygoing, unprejudiced readers there is, I believe, no great variation. Differences mount with sophistication—because the registering mind, so to say, comes to know too much. What happens is that our unforced sense of what is occurring is often complicated (and very naturally) by our sense of what Milton expects us to think is occurring. We know what he expects, partly from the information we bring to the poem, partly from the prods and reminders that Milton administers to us within it. In the upshot our reception of a given passage can be, and often is, a blend of two things: what we have really read in the passage, and what we know Milton is wishing us to read into it. But unless the two are kept distinct, and unless, in particular, we recognize that within the poem itself presentation and commentary may clash, we can make little headway, it seems to me, towards the truth about *Paradise Lost*.

The point, though simple, is of the first importance. I may illustrate it at once.

Mr C. S. Lewis in his chapter on Adam and Eve begins, as we have noted, by saying that for a long while he misunderstood Milton's intentions in regard to our first parents. Associating innocence with children he had expected an element of the childish in the portraits; and also, with his evolutionary background, he had come to the poem with vague pictures of early men ('and therefore *a fortiori* of the first men') as rather delightful savages. The beauty he looked for, he says, was that of 'the primitive, the unsophisticated, the *naif*'. I suppose few of us have not, at some time or other, been under a similar misconception.

It *is* a misconception of a sort, for in theory, at all events, Milton would appear to be imagining his Adam and Eve as two fully developed and perfected people. This, as Mr Lewis reminds us, was the view of Augustine: Adam's mental powers, said Augustine, 'surpassed those of the most brilliant philosopher as much as the speed of a bird surpasses that of a tortoise'. In other words, Adam was man *par excellence*, our flawless type and model, man as he ought always to have been, if he had not fallen away. And emphasizing all this, Mr Lewis dwells on that error, already mentioned, of Raleigh's. Raleigh, making mild fun of our forefather, had remarked that 'Adam from the depth of his inexperience is lavishly sententious': which, as Mr Lewis says, is rather to misrepresent Milton's idea. Adam, strictly, was never inexperienced; he had all knowledge, or at least the *pattern* of all knowledge, in his possession from the very beginning.

Mr Lewis then develops a fancy picture of what our sensations would have been like in the presence of two such people, supposing the Fall had never occurred: how once in a lifetime, perhaps, the opportunity would have come to us of making the great pilgrimage to the 'capital seat' of the earth; how 'after long journeys and ritual preparations and slow ceremonial approaches' we should have found ourselves at last before the great Father, Priest, and Emperor; how in that presence we should have stammered and shifted uneasily (Professor Raleigh is one of those, Mr Lewis thinks, who would have suffered a rude shock) for we should have felt ourselves to be in the presence of Royalty itself, the true type of something that Solomon and Charlemagne and Haroun-al-Raschid and Louis XIV strove all their lives unsuccessfully to imitate. In short (he makes his point) 'no useful criticism of the Miltonic Adam is possible until the last trace

of the *naif*, simple, childlike Adam has been removed from
our imaginations'. As a final proof that this couple, as
imagined by Milton, were really majestic and could sustain
without trouble their grandeur of manner Mr Lewis reminds
us that they uttered great verse extempore.

On technical grounds Mr Lewis's correction of Raleigh
no doubt has its point: Raleigh's remark was, in a sense,
a 'lapse'. And yet—we think of it again, and again we
smile, for the Adam of that remark *is* the Adam of the poem,
or, at the least, immeasurably closer to that Adam than the
Adam of Mr Lewis's imagining, who out-Charlemagned
Charlemagne. The position, surely, is perfectly clear. Adam
as conceived by Augustine and (it would seem) by Milton
is an Adam who simply cannot be shown.

This is not to deny that Adam has his moments, or that at
certain junctures he can be very impressive. Raleigh himself
admitted as much. It was Raleigh who used the phrase
'ambassadorial dignity' of Adam's bearing as he goes out
to meet the heavenly messenger. He keeps his poise, is not,
though modest and deferential, abashed. He goes

> not awd
> Yet with submiss approach and reverence meek,
> As to a superior Nature, bowing low.   (v, 358)

There is the scene again (IV, 720) in which with Eve he
stands adoring his Maker: the ritual act for the moment
sets the two apart from us and they take on a remoteness
of majesty. At such moments the effect of nobility and
loftiness that Milton perhaps was striving for was very nearly
secured. At such moments the Adam of the poem is very
close to the Adam that Milton had in mind. But how far
from such an Adam he often is! And how inevitable that
was! The test is too cruel. It was nearly as dangerous, in
a sense, to let Adam speak as to let God. If he passes the
time with gardening gossip he will sound stupid. If he
philosophizes he will sound—as Raleigh with perfect justice

says he sounds—sententious. If he lectures Eve on wifely
duties he will sound insufferably priggish. He adopts all
these tones, then finishes by sounding 'for all the world',
says Raleigh, 'as if he were a man of science lecturing to
some Philosophic Institute on the customs of savages'.[1] Mr
Lewis adjures us to remove from our criticism all impressions
of Adam that do not chime with the ideal picture that Milton
had in his mind. The answer, quite simply, is that we
cannot: to ask us to do such a thing is to forget for the
moment what literature is and what literature does. Adam,
conceived as St Augustine conceived him, can exist only
theoretically; he cannot exist in a poem.

With one proviso. Such a figure of flawless majesty, all-
wise, all-great, cannot be shown; but he could be *hinted*.
That, in fact, was precisely the method of Dante. Mr Lewis
himself refers to Dante's representation for proof of his own
argument. He translates the relevant passage:

> And Beatrice said, 'Within yon light
> The first of souls whom ever the First Cause
> Did make, with love beholds the God who made him.'
> Even as a leaf that in the passing wind
> Bows its frail head and, when the wind is passed,
> Of its own springy nature rises up,
> So did I bow my head (stupendous awe
> Was on me) while she spoke. But, strong desire
> To speak to him making me bold again,
> I soon began, 'O thou, the only fruit
> That came forth ripe and perfect.'   (*Paradiso*, XXVI, 83)

This, as Mr Lewis says, is the right note indeed. But how
is it struck? By an indirection. It is by a cunning obliqueness
that the effect is obtained. For the moment Dante (the
figure in the story) is overcome, and his emotion is transferred
to ourselves. That is the right, indeed the only, technique
for this special effect of unqualified wonder and awe: we
must *catch* it at second hand. Milton's problem was in

1 Op. cit. p. 250.

essentials the same, but it was not open to him to take Dante's way. He was compelled, as Dante was not, to set Adam properly going, make him talk; and the moment Adam begins to talk we become critical—we cannot help ourselves.

The point, though simple, is of such importance that I may perhaps be permitted to restate the moral of it, as it would seem to be brought out in Mr Lewis's approach. It is not to be thought, of course, that Mr Lewis does not receive the same impressions of Adam as Raleigh and the rest of us; but he has succeeded in developing a kind of immunity to them. As he writes he is not really thinking of the Adam of the poem; he is thinking of the visionary figure that floated before Augustine's eyes and also (though not, I would suggest, with the same clarity and intensity) before Milton's. Milton, Mr Lewis gathers, wished us to consider Adam as wise and great and kingly; very well, for Mr Lewis that settles the matter once and for all: Adam, whatever he may say or do, *is* wise and great and kingly. What Mr Lewis does, in short, is to apply to his impressions of Adam the drastic corrective of refusing to admit them; or, to put exactly the same thing in another way, he declines to acknowledge the facts of the poem.

Let us then in considering the Fall adopt a somewhat different plan, and while taking fully into account what Milton was intending to do, pay even more attention to what is after all the chief matter and our primary concern: what he has actually done.

We may begin with Eve, between whose fall and Adam's there is, I think, at least one radical difference: her fall, fairly seen, is a sequence: it is a train of events, not (as Adam's) one event.

It has been, although she does not know it, her unlucky day. Things have gone awry from the start. She wakes in independent mood; she decides to enjoy herself in her own fashion, to follow her whim, to set off, for once, alone. Adam's dissuasions merely strengthen her resolve to have, for this one time, her own way. Then she begins, unexpectedly, to enjoy the situation. Adam's opposition is a new experience, not without its interest. She begins to act a little, to play a part. She pretends to be hurt by his mistrust; she assumes an air of injured dignity:

> But that thou shouldst my firmness therefore doubt
> To God or thee, because we have a foe
> May tempt it, I expected not to hear.   (IX, 279)

She shows a pretty obstinacy, feels her power, gets her way. And then, hard on this triumph, while she is pleased with herself and flushed with success, come the sequences of the temptation: the serpent's compliment, his glozing words, his masterly mixing up of the issues, so that she is bewildered, and her fall.

But to separate the last act and call it exclusively by that name seems unfair. Mr Clarence Green has done this, and has concluded that there is an essential opposition between the fall of Eve and the fall of Adam. That the two falls are very different is obvious, but Mr Green would make a clean-cut philosophical distinction between them. 'Eve transgresses because her deceived mind misinforms her will, the subservient faculty. The account of her Fall is therefore intellectualistic: her *reason* is primary. Adam, however, transgresses "against his better knowledge, not deceav'd". The account of his Fall is voluntaristic: his *will* is primary.'[1] Superficially this might appear to fit the facts well enough; there is no doubt, at least, that in the fall of Eve reason is to the fore, as in the fall of Adam will is to the fore. All the same, Mr Green, I think, simplifies. He pictures Eve as a brave Humanist setting off on a praiseworthy expedition to seek out knowledge, 'the prerequisite of true virtue', wherever

[1] 'The Paradox of the Fall in *Paradise Lost*', *Modern Language Notes* (Dec. 1938), vol. LIII, pp. 563–4.

it may be found. 'Convinced of the "magic virtue of the fruit" she cannot "easily" abstain from eating. Indeed, *qua* Humanist she is bound not to abstain. The critics who have condemned Eve's conduct have done so at times a little too readily.'[1] And he says, with reference to Adam's fervid speech of warning (IX, 343) that it is 'tragically ironic that when Eve falls she does so, one may say, because she has been an attentive listener to Adam's Platonistic instruction; for her will obeys her reason, which has unfortunately been deceived, "surpris'd" by "a faire appeering good"'.[2]

Yes: but Adam's whole point is that reason must be ever on the watch—or that the will must keep it so. Reason in *Paradise Lost* is not imagined quite as Mr Green is imagining it here, as a kind of sensitive plate, essentially passive in its functioning, at the mercy of whatever impressions may come, so that if it happens to be clouded or 'deceived' in some way at a critical moment that is just our bad luck. Our task is to keep our reason in good condition, braced up and alert; it is our duty not to *allow* it to be caught napping; and it is precisely here that Eve, according to the poem, has failed. Mr Green says of Eve's reason that it 'has unfortunately been deceived'; but there is more in her reason's error than misfortune: that, at least, is what the poem is trying to say. Adam could not have been more insistent in his warnings:

> Reason he made right
> But bid her well beware, and still erect,
> Least by some faire appeering good surpris'd
> She dictate false....　　　　　　　　　(IX, 352)
>
> Firm we subsist, yet possible to swerve,
> Since Reason not impossibly may meet
> Some specious object by the Foe subornd,
> And fall into deception unaware,
> Not keeping strictest watch, as she was warnd.
> 　　　　　　　　　　　　　　　　(IX, 359)

1 Loc. cit. p. 568.
2 Ibid. p. 558.

Eve, it is true, is the weaker, her intellect in itself, we are to understand, more deceivable than Adam's. Even so, she has put herself at a disadvantage, she is caught—'our credulous Mother'—unawares. 'Her error', says Mr Green flatly, 'is intellectual, not moral.' But there is no one 'error': it is because of previous errors that she falls into her final error. Mr Green has seized on the last event of a chain of events, and even of that, I would suggest, has given a drastically simplified account. What he is giving, really, is a *diagram* of the Fall, and it is a diagram, I think, that misleads.[1]

To return to the sequence. There are four or five 'acts' or phases in the fall of Eve. The start, in a sense, is the dream. Ithuriel and Zephon have surprised Satan 'squat like a toad, close at the ear of Eve', busy injecting bad thoughts. In Eve's dream we see the results, mingled with harmless after-images of her last evening's conversation with Adam. It is a dream full of not very noxious vanities, the 'suppressed desires' in it (if we like to think of them that way) surely of no great moment. The angel who figured in it paid her pleasing compliments. He said:

> Happier thou mayst be, worthier canst not be.

He said:

> Taste this, and be henceforth among the Gods
> Thy self a Goddess; (v, 76)

---

1 Mr Green draws one kind of diagram, M. Saurat draws another. 'So in the story of the fall in the ixth book of *Paradise Lost*, Eve carried away by her feelings, which rule her only too easily, is blinded in her intellect, because her intellect is of an inferior quality. But Adam is not blinded. His fall comes because he, clear intelligence, allows Eve, blind passion, to lead.' (*Milton: Man and Thinker*, 1925, p. 160.) This is going as far in one direction as Mr Green goes in the other—or farther, for I do not think M. Saurat's summary contains one single statement that accords with our natural impressions of what occurs. Eve is not particularly 'ruled' by her feelings (Adam, when it comes to the point, is 'ruled' far more powerfully by his); she is not 'carried away', in the customary sense of this phrase; and if one of the two has to stand for 'blind passion' it had better again, surely, be Adam, though the truth is that the phrase will not do for either.

assuring her at the same time that if she had her deserts she
would be a goddess already. Adam, analysing her story, tells
her that in his opinion she has no great cause to worry, though
he notes that what she dreamt does contain 'addition strange'
—elements not quite accounted for by their last evening's
talk and the normal processes of 'mimic Fansie'. 'Yet be
not sad,' he says:

> Evil into the mind of God or Man
> May come and go, so unapprov'd, and leave
> No spot or blame behind.   (v, 117)

The second phase is her obstinacy on the fateful day, her
setting forth alone. One aspect of this seems interesting.
I would suggest that if we were obliged to choose from the
series of events constituting the double Fall one act (or failure
to act) of which we might quite fairly say that upon it the
whole issue depended, it would probably have to be Adam's
weakness here. It is perhaps the one single and specific piece
of behaviour having an absolutely critical importance. Later,
as we know, Eve makes it the occasion of explicit reproach:

> Being as I am, why didst not thou the Head
> Command me absolutely not to go,
> Going into such danger as thou saidst?
> Too facil then thou didst not much gainsay,
> Nay, didst permit, approve, and fair dismiss.
> Hadst thou bin firm and fixt in thy dissent,
> Neither had I transgress'd, nor thou with mee. (ix, 1155)

It is at this point that Adam first becomes 'incenst', and no
wonder, for it is the unkindest cut of all. At no point in the
poem is Milton himself more thoroughly *with* Adam than
at this; he is bitterly, weepingly with him. It is as if the two,
author and character, coalesce, and whose voice it is in that
final exasperated indictment we hardly know:

> Thus it shall befall
> Him who to worth in Women overtrusting
> Lets her Will rule; restraint she will not brook,
> And left to her self, if evil thence ensue,
> Shee first his weak indulgence will accuse.   (ix, 1182)

But the amusing thing is that Eve is perfectly right in her
contention: her position, on Adam's tenets and on Milton's
own, is absolutely unassailable. Just before he gave his
reluctant permission Adam had said:

> Trial will come unsought.
> Wouldst thou approve thy constancie, approve
> First thy obedience;   (IX, 366)

and he should immediately have seen to it that she did. The
point seems to me a pleasant one, but I have naturally no
intention of pressing it, and I presume that nobody, however
bent on tracking down the cause of the Fall to its farthest
lurking-place, will care to find the ultimate secret of it in
Adam's lack of firmness here.

The third phase is the temptation scene itself: one of the
great achievements, surely, of the poem. It is in itself a
sequence. There is first the overture—the 'proem'—by which
the tempter prepares the ground and makes a weakening in
Eve's defences, his chief weapon being flattery. 'Into the
heart of Eve his words made way.' He begins cautiously,
but presently finds that he need not stint his compliments
overmuch. Once or twice he oversteps the mark and she
counters neatly:

> Serpent, thy overpraising leaves in doubt
> The vertue of that Fruit, in thee first prov'd. (IX, 615)

But her curiosity is now thoroughly aroused; it would not
commit her, she feels, merely to *see* the tree; she asks how far
away it is and where it grows. This is the turning-point,
marked by that line which seems itself to exult:

> To whom the wilie Adder, blithe and glad.

There is more yet to do, but the game is as good as won, and
the tempter knows it as he eagerly leads the way. They come
to the tree and Eve's face falls, for it is the tree of prohibition
itself. Then we have the climax with the great temptation

speech. The serpent can scarcely wait for Eve to finish her objection. Full of what he has to say he

> Fluctuats disturbd, yet comely, and in act
> Rais'd, as of som great matter to begin,

as in olden days a famed orator of Athens or Rome would stand 'in himself collected',

> while each part,
> Motion, each act won audience ere the tongue,
> Sometimes in highth began, as no delay
> Of Preface brooking through his Zeal of Right.
> So standing, moving, or to highth upgrown,
> The Tempter all impassiond thus began.   (IX, 668)

The speech itself is a feat not so much of logic as of legerdemain. It is crammed with specious argument, with sequences that look like syllogisms but stop before they have arrived, with stretches of reasoning that sound as if they are reaching a conclusion but do not quite reach it; and the ground is shifted every few seconds. What seems the same argument has turned in the twinkling of an eye into one that is really its opposite. It is a flashing string of incompatibilities, a glittering exhibition of plausible thought and spurious logic; and Eve, naturally, is bewildered. It is asking altogether too much of her to expect her to sort out and classify the fallacies in such a speech while she is listening to it. She has no more chance of *thinking out* what the tempter is saying than most of us have of detecting the flaws in what a bond salesman is telling us—while he is telling us. Our only defence (as hers would have been) is a closed mind. And that, of course, is the point: her mind has been opened: his words have 'too easie entrance' won.[1]

1 The movement of the thought is very interesting. There is the brilliant suggestion that the prohibition may be a trick of God's to test their courage, for if they risk death ('whatever thing Death be') to achieve knowledge of Good and Evil they will have earned their Creator's praise indeed. If God punishes for this he will not be just; but if he is not just, how can he be God? So, momentarily, God is argued away. But the

This is nearly the end. The fruit by this time is fascinating her: she gazes on it 'fixt' while the specious reasoning still sounds in her ears, and as she looks her senses begin to stir. But before she plucks it she does one more thing: she pauses and thinks. She thinks hard and she thinks well. Logically what she says to herself holds together much better than the speech of the tempter: her reasoning is quite sound. Unfortunately it all happens to be based on a false premise, the premise, namely, that the serpent, in imputing various changes in himself to the fruit, spoke truth. She sees the facts of the serpent's present condition—startling enough. Somewhat excusably she accepts his account of them; and on that acceptance her reasoning is based. As she eats (as she is in the very process of 'falling') an idea flits into her mind that connects what is occurring at this minute with the dream that began it all, and binds the whole sequence together. We are told: 'nor was God-head from her thought'. (IX, 790).

What, then, is the meaning of it? Can we *define* the fall of Eve, express it in a formula?

There have been many attempts. Some, I think, we may dismiss easily. Sensuality, for example, of which M. Saurat makes so much, hardly enters into the question here, unless we are willing to count in that way her eager appetite, raised by the smell

> So savorie of that Fruit. (IX, 740)

Any inclusive theory of the Fall, therefore, that derives it from sensuality would seem to be out of court.

The late Mr Charles Williams found the key in 'injured merit', which had the advantage of linking this part at least of the story of the Fall with the story of Satan. Satan

next moment he is back again, this time not as the God who may be testing them in an unexpected way, but in quite a different guise, as a God jealous of them, bent on keeping them down. God keeps slipping in and out of the argument like this and undergoes lightning changes in the process.

certainly fell because of a sense of injured merit, and what the tempter stirs up in Eve, says Mr Williams, is very much the same thing: 'a sense of proper dignity, of self-admiration, of rights withheld, of injured merit.'[1] It is ultimately a 'self-loving spirit' that brings about her doom.

No one would deny, I suppose, that the tempter has succeeded in awakening in Eve some of the feelings that Mr Williams mentions. The tempter does, to some extent, give her a sense of rights withheld, he does appeal to her self-admiring spirit, to some extent he does, perhaps, awake in her a sense of injured merit. But an experiment along these lines would be interesting. Select some candid person, reasonably well informed, and read out to him the expressions used by Mr Williams: sense of proper dignity, of self-admiration, of rights withheld, of injured merit. Then let such a person write down noted names in history or fiction that pop into his head. One could predict, I imagine, with nearly absolute certainty, two results, one positive, one negative: the name of Satan *would* be on such a list, the name of Eve would not.

This suggests that Mr Williams is simplifying, making, for the benefit of a general theory of *Paradise Lost* that very much appeals to him, an artificial abstraction from the total truth. Indeed, it would not be easy, I think, to compile a thoroughly satisfactory catalogue of the various elements in Eve's experience before her fall and the various aspects of her behaviour. One might make out a long list and still feel that one had not, perhaps, come to the end of all that might be set down. There is frivolity in her conduct (in the sense that she follows a whim); there is wilfulness (in the sense that she persists in the whim); there is vanity; there is a measure of stupidity (though not very much); there is mild ambition (in the sense that she has, if we like to put it so, the instincts of a social climber: she does not quite see, once

1 Loc. cit. p. xiv.

the delectable alternative has been pointed out to her, why she should spend all her days in Eden); there is, as Mr Williams says, a feeling of injured merit (but not, surely, in the sense that she has a grudge; *her* feeling of injured merit has been in her heart for about two minutes and might as quickly go out again); and there is curiosity. And I am not sure, if we are to choose one of these words and spell it with a capital letter, that it ought not to be the last. I feel that that would be on the whole a juster proceeding than to make all hinge on Pride.

That is what Mr Lewis does. Mr Williams merely slipped in 'pride', not applying it very directly to Eve; Mr Lewis picks out the word and capitalizes it. 'The Fall is simply and solely Disobedience—doing what you have been told not to do: and it results from Pride—from being too big for your boots, forgetting your place, thinking that you are God.'[1] The second of these two statements seems to me as false to the impressions of the poem as the first is true to them: false because it strives to put into a formula what will not go into one. Eve, it is perfectly true, breaks union, asserts her independence, insists on selfhood (the thing that Mr Lewis and Mr Williams are against), has an impulse, as Mr Lewis expresses it, to be 'on her own'. If all this equals pride, then Eve, very plainly, is proud. But does it? Of course if we are taking the word in a purely theological way, there is perhaps little more to be said. Augustine's 'pride' (*esse in semet ipso*) is of a reference so broad that it is difficult to conceive of any independent human activity that might not arguably be brought under the ban. But Mr Lewis would seem in at least much of his discussion to be using 'pride' as a descriptive modern term. He takes as a motto for one chapter:

> Maysterful mod and highe pryde
> I hete thee, arn heterly hated here.[2]

---

1 Op. cit. p. 69.   2 Ibid. p. 65.

Pride, he says, is 'forgetting your place, thinking that you are God'. Such phrases fit Satan to perfection. But in that case are we not justified in asking: if they fit Satan how *can* they, with whatever tugging and straining, fit poor pitiful Eve? Even if we think of a scale of proud people with Satan at the top of it and Eve at the bottom, still the word will hardly do. It is far too mighty a word for her, and that is why Mr Williams in speaking of her tactfully avoids it.

What else is left? Always in the background, of course, is the radical opposition—in theory at least—between 'reason' and 'passion', and I suppose Milton's scheme would almost oblige us to regard passion (in his technical sense) as colouring Eve's behaviour. Without some partial victory of passion over reason it is difficult, strictly, to see how sin could occur. We might perhaps put it that she sins through her passion-impregnated reason. But in her case the impregnation is very small, and of passion in our customary sense she displays, of course, hardly a trace. She is not impetuous, she is not emotional, she is not carried away. As Dr Tillyard remarks, she shows little strength of feeling. Before the fatal step she pauses and considers again.

Dr Tillyard himself has a word. He admits the variety of her feelings but thinks they may be gathered up under the head 'levity' or 'triviality of mind'; and no doubt if we *are* to have a word, that meets the case as well as another. But is even that quite satisfactory? Does Eve, in her final earnest debate with herself, show levity? I do not think so. I would suggest that there is no word. And if that is so, what is the inference? The inference, I think, is that Milton's mind was much less set on the *causes* of the Fall than one would judge from many discussions of the poem. He has his general theory of passion conquering reason: a somewhat loose conceptual framework, when all is said, as we may see from the difficulty of making any rigorous application of it to Eve. And when he comes to particulars, he works, it would seem, very much as an opportunist. There are lines that he must follow, but the filling in is largely a matter for his own selection, and as the details come to him he is not at every moment thinking of their rigid fitness for a thesis. His thesis (despite the accumulation of critical commentary upon it) would appear to be very simple. His point of points, as Mr Lewis says, is the disobedience: *that* is the thesis, that is the meaning towards which he continually drives. How the disobedience came about, what was behind it, was not (I would suggest again) a concern of nearly such grave import to Milton as the inquiries into this problem, from Greenlaw down, would lead one to think. The proof would seem to be, first: that it is extremely difficult to find a satisfactory formula for the fall of Eve; and second: that it is utterly impossible to find a formula that will do for her fall and for the fall of Adam as well.

This brings us to some of the most interesting critical problems of the poem.

CHAPTER III

THE FALL (II)

THE preparations for the crisis of the poem, the fall of Adam, go some way back, and I think if we examine them closely we may detect the beginnings of a slight uncertainty on Milton's part: faint premonitory hesitations and inconsistencies that tell of trouble ahead. I do not suggest that Milton was even yet, except vaguely, aware of trouble ahead; but it is now, in the presentation of Adam's fall, that those deep underlying ambiguities in the theme begin to make themselves really felt, like subterranean weaknesses that all at once start the earth cracking at the surface. Rifts begin to open, hair lines at first; then they become wider, and presently there is a chasm.

We may detect such symptoms and signals, I think, in one speech especially, the speech towards the end of Book VIII that Raphael delivers 'with contracted brow'. Raphael in what he says here is obviously Milton's spokesman: he, and Milton behind him, feel that they have some highly important principles to lay down. The principles are, in fact, to serve as foundation for what ensues; their function is to support the poem across its most critical phase. But Raphael does his work rather clumsily and gives us little confidence that his props will hold.

Adam has been telling how in Taste, Sight, Smell he finds pleasure indeed, but pleasure not comparable to the 'commotion strange' that the presence of Eve has power to awaken. His own speech is a curious mixture. At one moment he merely mouths his author's theories of woman's place and function:

> For well I understand in the prime end
> Of Nature her th' inferiour, in the mind
> And inward Faculties, which most excell. (VIII, 540)

At another, his tribute is so deep and moving that one can
hardly relate it to the tone with which he seemed to begin—
the tone of one who is

> in all enjoyments else
> Superiour and unmov'd, here onely weake
> Against the charm of Beauties powerful glance.
>
> (VIII, 532)

'Beauties powerful glance': the phrase is oddly discordant
with the final lines of the passage in which Adam, speaking
from the heart, tells us what he really feels:

> when I approach
> Her loveliness, so absolute she seems
> And in her self compleat, so well to know
> Her own, that what she wills to do or say,
> Seems wisest, vertuousest, discreetest, best;
> All higher knowledge in her presence falls
> Degraded, Wisdom in discourse with her
> Looses discount'nanc't, and like folly shewes;
> Authoritie and Reason on her waite,
> As one intended first, not after made
> Occasionally; and to consummate all,
> Greatness of mind and nobleness thir seat
> Build in her loveliest, and create an awe
> About her, as a guard Angelic plac't. (VIII, 546)

If the first half of Adam's testimony—in which he speaks
of his nature's one 'weakness'—expresses Milton, so also of
course does this half, and profoundly. But then Milton
checks himself and makes the angel contract his brow.

Raphael's is an unpleasant speech; more than that, it is
an untruthful one. It begins:

> Accuse not Nature, she hath don her part;
> Do thou but thine, and be not diffident
> Of Wisdom, she deserts thee not, if thou
> Dismiss not her, when most thou needst her nigh,
> By attributing overmuch to things
> Less excellent, as thou thy self perceav'st.

And then:

> For what admir'st thou, what transports thee so,
> An outside? fair no doubt, and worthy well

> Thy cherishing, thy honouring, and thy love,
> Not thy subjection: weigh with her thy self;
> Then value: Oft times nothing profits more
> Then self-esteem, grounded on just and right
> Well manag'd; of that skill the more thou know'st,
> The more she will acknowledge thee her Head,
> And to realities yeild all her shows.   (VIII, 561)

Raphael's technique, that is to say, is to ignore everything in what Adam has just said that is at all inconvenient for his own particular purpose. Having suppressed all that, he then takes what is left of Adam's speech and replies to it.

> For what admir'st thou, what transports thee so,
> An outside?

All Adam's qualifications have gone for naught: the whole of that extremely important *supplement* which ended his speech has fallen on deaf ears—or ears which have been deliberately deafened.

> And to realities yeild all her shows.

Once more Raphael wilfully misses the point. After which he proceeds to his homily on 'the sense of touch', still blandly assuming that there is no more in question, though the whole drift of Adam's confession has been to prove that there is a very great deal more in question. And then, having in this way completely reversed the proportions of Adam's speech he gives him permission to go on loving 'what higher' in Eve's society he finds, and concludes by explaining to him (as if there were need, for what has Adam been doing himself but giving the plainest possible exposition of this very thing?) 'wherein true love consists'.

Adam, 'half-abash't', though there is no reason why he should be, ventures on a reply. It is a good reply, and makes doubly clear what is already clear. Raphael has just said that

> love refines
> The thoughts, and heart enlarges.   (VIII, 589)

Listen to Adam:

> Neither her out-side formd so fair, nor aught
> In procreation common to all kindes
> (Though higher of the genial Bed by far,
> And with mysterious reverence I deem)
> So much delights me, as those graceful acts,
> Those thousand decencies that daily flow
> From all her words and actions, mixt with Love
> And sweet compliance, which declare unfeign'd
> Union of Mind, or in us both one Soule.   (VIII, 596)

May not one fairly suggest that a man who speaks like this
has already had his thoughts refined and his heart enlarged
—is already passing Raphael's tests tolerably well? Adam
ends by protesting that he is not in 'subjection'—that that
is not quite the right word for his state—and hints meekly
that the angel's strictures may have been a little unfair.

Let us come now to the climax: the climax of the story
of Adam and Eve, and of course also of the whole poem.
Eve, running towards Adam excitedly and covering up her
nervousness in a flow of rapid and eager speech, tells him
what she has done.

It is, I think, of great importance to note *exactly* what
happens now. Adam stands thunderstruck, 'amaz'd' and
'blank,'

> while horror chill
> Ran through his veins, and all his joynts relax'd.
>
> (IX, 890)

And then:

> First to himself he inward silence broke.   (IX, 895)

Before saying a word to Eve, that is, he communes with
himself, and in doing so he accepts at once and completely
two facts: first, she is lost; and second, he is lost with her.
For he has decided on the instant, without thinking, without
having to think, that that is how it is to be:

> And mee with thee hath ruind, for with thee
> Certain my resolution is to Die.   (IX, 907)

It is to be observed that Eve has had no chance as yet to coax or persuade; within the first few appalled moments Adam has come uninfluenced to his resolve. I would suggest that the nine lines that complete this speech (the speech of self-communion) and the eight lines that complete the next (Adam's first speech to Eve after the shock of the news) are in many respects the two most important passages in *Paradise Lost*.

The first passage goes:

> How can I live without thee, how forgoe
> Thy sweet Converse and Love so dearly joyn'd
> To live again in these wilde Woods forlorn?
> Should God create another *Eve*, and I
> Another Rib afford, yet loss of thee
> Would never from my heart; no, no, I feel
> The Link of Nature draw me; Flesh of Flesh,
> Bone of my Bone thou art, and from thy State
> Mine never shall be parted, bliss or woe. (IX, 908)

How shall we interpret this? By what word shall we describe the feeling in the lines? There is apprehended loneliness in them, of course. In the several furious seconds that have passed since the disclosure the future has had time to flash on Adam in some of its implications. But dread of solitariness is only part of what these words convey. If Adam's words are permitted to have the meanings that words usually have in English, these lines mean *love*: I do not see how it is possible to withhold the word; and the lines that echo them a few seconds later mean the same.

In between comes what Mr Clarence Green has well called Adam's 'rationalizing' speech. It is the speech in which, a little 'recomforted from sad dismay', he tries to persuade himself that things may not be as bad as they seem. He only half believes what he is saying even while he is saying it. Then (with the effect of putting aside these 'perhapses') comes the significant word 'however', and the transition to the second full avowal of purpose.

However I with thee have fixt my Lot
Certain to undergoe like doom, if Death
Consort with thee, Death is to mee as Life;
So forcible within my heart I feel
The Bond of Nature draw me to my owne,
My own in thee, for what thou art is mine;
Our State cannot be severd, we are one,
One Flesh; to loose thee were to loose my self.

(IX, 952)

I would emphasize again the very great importance of these two passages. They demonstrate to us what Adam's feelings are as he takes his fateful decision—they are our prime, paramount evidence for those feelings—and I would suggest, therefore, that we should allow no one, *not even Milton*, to prise us loose from them or in any way to diminish for us their natural significance. Dr Tillyard says that Adam's first thought was of 'comradeship': that he cannot bear the thought of being alone, and that that is why he determines to die with Eve. 'Comradeship' and Dr Tillyard's companion word 'gregariousness' seem to me to hover timidly on the mere fringe of the truth. Adam wants company, that is certain; but he does not want the company of anyone, even the company of another Eve; it is *this* Eve he wants: he says so. 'Adam', says Mr Lewis, 'fell by uxoriousness.' Is Adam uxorious? Perhaps. In his love, as in anyone's love, there are many strains. There is protectiveness in it, there is loyalty, there is (very pronounced) what Augustine called the 'drawing of kindred', and no doubt there is uxoriousness. His life with Eve up to this point has had the air of an extended honeymoon—which is very much, of course, what it really has been. To say that he is 'in love' with her is to use a mild expression. But at this supreme moments, when life and death hang in the balance, the garland-weaving and all that it signifies are beside the point. When he decides, on his own impulse, at once and finally, to share her fate, are we to call *this* uxorious? The word (to me at least) seems fantastically

xcessively or submissively fond of a wife

trivial for a description of the deep movements of feeling
that those two critical passages convey.

The second passage comes, as just noted, at the end of
Adam's 'rationalizing' speech. I think that Dr Tillyard is
less than fair to the impression of this speech when he says
that it shows Adam falling into mental levity. Adam is
serious enough underneath. The speech is a desperate attempt
to put the best face on things. In a natural reaction from the
horror of the first few moments Adam brightens a little; the
decision that he has taken is in itself invigorating. But he has
no real faith in what he is saying, as the transitional word
'however' sufficiently suggests.

And it will be observed (Dr Tillyard himself emphasizes
the point) that not even yet has Eve had to say a word of
persuasion: there has been no need. Of course now that she
has heard from Adam's own lips what he means to do she
is deeply moved and behaves as any woman would, embracing
him and weeping tenderly and pouring out her gratitude in
words. With a natural uprush of optimism she says that she
is sure all will be well, and then offers him the fruit. But
the grand, the controlling decision has already been taken.

Now comes a question that must be asked and answered.
If all this is so, what then does Milton mean a line or two
later when he tells us that Adam was 'fondly overcome with
Femal charm'?

> She gave him of that fair enticing Fruit
> With liberal hand: he scrupl'd not to eat
> Against his better knowledge, not deceav'd,
> But fondly overcome with Femal charm.   (IX, 996)

Dr Tillyard notes the discrepancy: 'the last line is curiously
inconsistent with what went before.'[1] I think it is: 'fondly
overcome with Femal charm', take it as broadly as we will,
is oddly out of harmony with what we have just been reading,
and especially with the two key passages that have revealed

1 *Milton*, p. 263.

to us the motions of Adam's heart. Dr Tillyard sees in the inconsistency a plain shift of motive: from his point of view the shift is one from 'gregariousness' to 'sensuality'; and his conclusion, therefore, is that Adam's 'final sin' is uxoriousness after all.

This, it seems to me, is to submit too meekly to Milton's leading, to abdicate far too many of our critical rights. That there is a shift of some sort is unquestionable, but it is not, I think, the kind of shift that Dr Tillyard has in mind. That would be to take the lines under discussion far too seriously, and the lines that have gone before not seriously enough. We have here, I would suggest, a perfect illustration of the principle noted at the beginning of the previous chapter, a perfect example of the sort of clash that we must sometimes expect in *Paradise Lost* between Milton's theory of a matter and the matter as he has actually presented it. This is, indeed, one of *the* moments in the poem for bringing that distinction to bear. 'Fondly overcome with Femal charm' is simply Milton's comment on the recent course of events: events the true nature of which he has just been demonstrating to us. And between a comment and a demonstration (though in the critical interpretation of *Paradise Lost* it has been nearly the rule, I suppose, to accord them equal rights) there can never be real question, surely, which has the higher validity. 'Femal charm' is merely Milton's way of inciting us to take a certain view of a matter that he has already presented with a quite different emphasis and to a quite different effect. What the comment really means is that Milton has begun to realize, if vaguely, that his material has been getting out of hand. He is rather like a steersman who, feeling the ship off her course and yawing, puts the helm hard over to bring her back: except that he is not quite as conscious of what is happening to his poem as a steersman would be of what was happening to his ship, and that his action is too late. For the 'harm' (if we like to look at it that way) is done. As

long as those two key passages remain in the poem their
effect cannot be neutralized (unless of course we permit
ourselves to be levered out of all our critical rights). Adam's
words ring so true that they *prove* to us his feelings, and against
proof of that kind no comment can—or ought to—prevail.
To accept Adam's final sin as uxoriousness, on the authority
of this belated and tendentious summing up of his case, is
merely, I would suggest, to allow Milton to lead us by the nose.

If anyone should feel that such a reading commits Milton
to an improbable inconsistency let him consider merely the
disagreements in the sequel. Adam presently is brought to
book: he has to give an account of his deed to the Son. And
it is very curious to note what happens at this interview.
Adam is his own worst possible advocate. His testimony
is unfair to himself and to Eve and amounts to a nearly
total misrepresentation of what really occurred. He is silent
about the extremely honourable motives that prompted him,
and he puts Eve in a much worse light than is necessary by
declaring that from her hand he could 'suspect no ill'—a
flat lie, which at once lays additional discredit on her and
deprives his own conduct of the nobility it possessed.
Altogether, it is a miserable, hang-dog performance. It may
be said that we are meant to see in this mean-spirited
exhibition one of the earliest results of the Fall itself. But it
is interesting to note that the Son accepts the account, takes
Adam at his word, so that the version becomes from now on,
in a sense, the official view of the poem.

> To whom the sovran Presence thus repli'd.
> Was shee thy God, that her thou didst obey
> Before his voice, or was shee made thy guide.... (x, 144)

Adam did not 'obey' Eve, and she was not his 'guide'.

What then shall we say of the central event of *Paradise Lost*?
Dr Tillyard points the paradox. On the one hand, 'the heart
of any normal reader warms with sympathy at [those]
exquisitely tender words of Adam refusing to forsake Eve

in her extremity'. On the other, 'how can Milton at this of all places in the poem have given Adam his conscious approval?' And any other kind of 'approval', at such a crucial point as this, seems to Dr Tillyard difficult to accept. His conclusion is that we must make the best we can of what seems to be Milton's meaning, which is that 'ordinary man is far too weak to live alone'. Adam, owing to 'gregariousness', has sinned.[1]

I do not feel that this is quite the way out. Dr Tillyard, I think, is inclined to overestimate Milton's *awareness* of what is occurring. If one impression rather than another grows stronger with each reading of *Paradise Lost* it is (I would suggest again) that Milton is by no means always alive to the precise effect that his narrative is making and to the exact way in which parts of it interlock with other parts; and indeed, without going farther afield at the moment for examples, the glaring inconsistencies just noted are themselves ample proof. We have, I think, to remind ourselves that the presentation of the Fall was one of the severest tests for Milton in the poem; in many ways it was *the* test. The hidden difficulties of the theme can at this point remain hidden no longer; the lurking problems must now become apparent, even if they are still not faced. I do not think it can be said that Milton faces them: he is not, even here, in any proper sense aware of them. What he does is to yield himself, at the critical moments, to the full imaginative promptings of his subject. The treatment of the fall of Adam, in the passages I have so much emphasized, is a noble and generous treatment, and the whole account of the Fall is studded with true and memorable things. Only, there is the thesis in the background; he cannot forever neglect it; hence 'Femal charm'.

The matter then may be summed up quite bluntly by saying that Adam falls through love—not through sensuality,

1 Op. cit. p. 262

not through uxoriousness, not (above all) through gregariousness—but through love as human beings know it at its best,
through true love, through the kind of love that Raphael has
told Adam

> is the scale
> By which to heav'nly Love thou maist ascend.   (VIII, 591)

This fact is not usually faced (one of the few who dare to
speak of Adam's 'love' is Mr Green) but it is almost uni-
versally felt. It is difficult to find a critic of *Paradise Lost* who
(however shattering to his scheme of the poem the admission
may be) will not confess, as Dr Tillyard does, that his heart is
warmed at Adam's act. M. Saurat, though the consequences
of what he is saying do not, I think, quite strike him, concedes
that Milton has a sense of chivalry: 'what greater instance in
the whole world than that of Adam deliberately and clear-
headedly joining Eve in her transgression, not to be parted
from her in the punishment?'[1] 'When Adam', writes Mr
Williams, 'in the fullness of his passion for Eve, really does
abandon heaven and his knowledge of God for her, Milton
denounced his act. But it was, after all, Milton who imagined
his passion so intensely as to make us almost wish it could be
approved.'[2] Mr Williams will not quite say 'love', but
'fullness of passion' is a periphrasis for it. And even Mr Lewis,
though somewhat frowningly, admits the 'half-nobility' of
what Adam did. Everybody admits it; Milton himself by
the sympathy and warmth of his presentment (not his
comment) implicitly admits it. And yet this noble (or at
the very least 'half-noble') act constitutes the Fall of Man.

What are we to say? Mr Lewis has his answer ready, and
if this answer will not do, none will. 'If the reader', he says,
'finds it hard to look upon Adam's action as a sin at all, that
is because he is not really granting Milton's premises.' He
explains his point. 'If conjugal love were the highest value
in Adam's world, then of course his resolve would have been

1 Op. cit. p. 169.   2 Loc. cit. p. xvii.

the correct one. But if there are things that have an even higher claim on a man, if the universe is imagined to be such that, when the pinch comes, a man ought to reject wife and mother and his own life also, then the case is altered, and then Adam can do no good to Eve (as, in fact, he does no good) by becoming her accomplice.'[1]

Before commenting on this I cannot forbear pointing out what it is that Mr Lewis is really asking of us when he suggests that we ought to wish that Adam had acted 'correctly'. He is asking us to wish that Adam had been, not Adam, but Sir Charles Grandison. 'Do you think, my dear,' asks Miss Harriet Byron of her correspondent (she is talking of Sir Charles), 'that had he been the first man, he would have been so complaisant to his Eve as Milton makes Adam [So contrary to that part of his character, which made him accuse the woman to the Almighty]—To taste the forbidden fruit, because he would not be separated from her, in her punishment, though all posterity were to suffer by it?—No; it is my opinion, that your brother would have had gallantry enough to his fallen spouse, to have made him extremely regret her lapse; but that he would have done his own duty, were it but for the sake of posterity, and left it to the Almighty, if such had been his pleasure, to have annihilated his first Eve and given him a second.'[2] (It will be observed that Miss Byron has noted the striking contrast, to say the least of it, between the Adam who acted and the Adam who bore false witness against himself—and Eve—before the Almighty.)

Mr Lewis's argument, though it sounds plausible, will not, I think, stand up under examination. Let us imagine an extreme instance. Suppose we take, as a premise, that Might is Right, that it is proper for the weak to be pushed to the wall; and suppose that a writer, adopting this premise, concocts a short story about a lifeboat. In this story the men

1 Op. cit. p. 123.
2 *Sir Charles Grandison* (Shakespeare Head Edition, vol. IV, p. 362).

first fight amongst themselves, then the strongest, who are the ones left, grab the food and push the women and children overboard. We should not particularly enjoy such a story, and we should feel that the answer, 'Oh, but you must grant the premises', had overlooked something. I think that what it would have overlooked would have been an unbearable collision of values, for we could not concede *that* value without conceding virtually all—without anæsthetizing, temporarily, nine-tenths of our emotional nature. There are limits to what, in literature, can be conceded as premises. A simple instance is the beginning of *The Pilgrim's Progress*: we are near the danger line there, if indeed we have not crossed it. For Bunyan, theoretically, would not have us abandon our customary human values—his allegory, like every allegory, owes its very point to an acceptance of those human values —yet he comes very near in this passage to affronting some of the chief of them. Christian running across the plain, his fingers in his ears to shut out the cries of his wife and children, desperately bent on his own salvation, is not the kind of person for whom in normal circumstances we should have a strong regard. Though we understand perfectly what Bunyan is driving at we cannot very much enjoy the scene: we are forced, as we read it, to suspend a great many of our customary emotional responses. A child does not so easily do this and is likely to be taken aback, feeling in some vague way that the situation tugs against itself. It does; and so, on a much bigger scale, does the central situation of *Paradise Lost*.

Our predicament is this, that we are asked to set aside, to discount for the moment—not some trifling prejudice, not some new light modern fancy or custom—but one of the highest, and really one of the oldest, of all human values: selflessness in love. This is not merely one of *our* values: it is just as certainly one of Milton's values. And we must set this aside, keep it in abeyance while we read, suppress it—

for what? It is by no means enough to set over against this powerful human value the mere doctrine that God must be obeyed: a mere doctrine can never counterbalance it, and Milton, theoretically, knows that as well as anyone. That, in fact, is precisely why he has written *Paradise Lost*: to *prove* the doctrine that God at all times and in all circumstances must be obeyed—to prove this in the only way in which a poet can prove anything, by bringing it home to our imaginations, by making us feel it, not in the abstract, but immediately, in the situation as shown, with all the conditions of that situation pressing strongly upon us. It is perfectly true, as Mr Lewis says, that 'pinches' come in life when a man ought to put his wife or family second, to leave them, perhaps, to death. The principle of the 'higher claim', from numberless treatments of it, is perfectly familiar to us. But the whole point surely is that we must be made to realize that there is a 'pinch'. Does any reader, responding naturally (as he ought to, for Milton has written his poem with the precise object of enlisting our natural responses) feel that such a pinch has arisen here? Adam seems to us—he seems to Milton, although Milton is not in a position to admit it— to be doing a worthy thing. Against the law, against what is theoretically good, against God, he deliberately asserts what is for him a higher good and pursues it.

It is not true, I think, to say (as is sometimes said) that we are here concerned with what is a normal thing after all in literature, the typical tragic conflict. The case seems very different. The conflict here is in us: it is we who are pulled in two ways, who are denied the full-hearted response that a great tragic theme allows and compels. For it is not as if the thesis of the poem were in the slightest degree in doubt. The poem thrusts on us a view, insists on an attitude. The assumption that Adam is to be condemned is basic: the whole of *Paradise Lost* rests on it. Yet, because of the nature of the presentation, we cannot condemn him: that is the kind of conflict in which we are caught. We should be watchful of apparent analogies. A woman in real life shelters her deserter husband; the court imposes the lightest of sentences, sympathizing with the woman and seeing that she could not have done otherwise. Here, in a sense, we both condemn and approve. But the conflict is nominal: we decide at once where the higher claim lies. The conflict in our response to *Paradise Lost* is far from nominal. If we push analysis to the limit we find, I think, that it comes to this: the poem asks from us, at one and the same time, two incompatible responses. It requires us, not tentatively, not half-heartedly (for there can be no place really for half-heartedness here) but with the full weight of our minds to believe that Adam did right, and simultaneously requires us with the full weight of our minds to believe that he did wrong. The dilemma is as critical as that, and there is no way of escape.

It does not help very much to imagine what Adam might have done; almost anything he might have done would have been less attractive than what he did. He might, for example (it is a suggestion of Mr Lewis's), have 'scolded or even chastised Eve and then interceded with God on her behalf'.[1] He might, though it seems hardly fair to blame him for taking God at his word. But if he had adopted this line, what then? Should we prefer even this Adam to the Adam we have? Would we rather that *he* had been our representative than the Adam who impulsively, uselessly, nobly stood by Eve and accepted, without further ado, her fate?

There is no way out. *Paradise Lost* cannot take the strain at its centre, it breaks there, the theme is too much for it. And it does not help very much to say that such a breakdown was unavoidable, though I suppose there is no question that it was. The myth of the Fall was dangerous, and the more intensely it was imagined the more dangerous it became. If Milton, in imagining it intensely and writing it large,

1 Op. cit. p. 123.

succeeded only (as in a sense surely he did) in reaching a result the exact opposite of what he had intended: if the net effect of all his labour is to justify man's ways against God's ways: well, that was one of the risks, inherent in the venture, that he did not see.

I make one further observation, returning for a moment to that quest for the 'real theme' that so preoccupied Greenlaw and since then has exercised Dr Tillyard, the late Mr Williams and others. If it is necessary (as I suggest it is) to yield the mind with all the naturalness possible to the impressions of the narrative as they come, it is just as necessary, surely, to listen to Milton when he tells us what he is driving at, and to believe him. Now Milton says that his theme is disobedience, and the woe that came of it. Disobedience, woe; disobedience, woe; the words are paired a hundred times in the poem. It does not lessen the difficulties to go behind this announced theme, believing that it is too naïve to be possible: it increases them. For example, everyone feels that the punishment of Adam and Eve is harsh. But does it do much good to probe into the causes of the disobedience in an attempt to find some offence in the background that will render the doom less disproportionate? Dr Tillyard has probed, and what has he found? Gregariousness, levity. These are the horrors for which our first parents are *really* being punished. 'Feebly they commit what they imagine is a trifling error, for which they are punished with a doom out of all apparent proportion to their crime. To their crime, yes; but not to the mental triviality that accompanied it: by their miserable inadequacy before the issues of life mankind have deserved their fate.'[1] (I think there is a fallacy here, embodied in the phrase 'issues of life'. The reasonless taboo does not, surely, represent an issue of life in any real sense: if it had, then mankind perhaps would have deserved its fate.) But, in any case, is levity a better cause for the awful doom than outright

1 Op. cit. p. 289.

disobedience? Has Dr Tillyard helped matters by looking beneath the disobedience and finding—gregariousness?

It is interesting, again (it is another aspect of the same matter) to note what happens to those inquiries, like Greenlaw's or Mr Williams's, or, in fact, Dr Tillyard's own, that attempt to trace the Fall to some single unifying principle. I have already referred to Greenlaw's article, 'A Better Teacher than Aquinas'. Greenlaw's view, in essence, was that the central philosophy of the poem is 'from Greece, not from Genesis', seeing that choice (upon which obedience or disobedience depends) 'involves abstaining through temperance, the rational principle of the soul, or yielding through excess, the irrational principle'.[1] Adam fell because the irrational principle in his soul, inflamed by a provoking object, triumphed over temperance, not because he disobeyed, as Raleigh said, 'a whimsical Tyrant'. Greenlaw guards himself to some extent by insisting that the conception of σωφροσύνη which Milton takes over from Spenser is Platonic, not Aristotelian, and means not merely temperance as absence of excess, a golden mean, but also 'the control of all powers, mental desires as well as physical desires, by the rational element in the soul'.[2] So qualified it ceases, of course, to be our own or even Milton's 'temperance' in any strict sense at all, and it is doubtful whether Greenlaw has a right to keep on using the English word. He does, however, and the impression that his article makes as a whole is certainly that we have to do with an opposition between 'moderation' and 'excess', and that this opposition is central to Milton's meaning. I need not linger further on this article. Part of its purpose was to establish a 'humanistic' Milton, and at the time it was unquestionably of great service in drawing attention to aspects of Milton's nature that had rather dropped out of sight. It more than redressed the balance, for one would have been hard put to it to gather from Greenlaw's

1 Loc. cit. pp. 200–1.   2 Ibid. p. 211.

discussion that Milton had ever been a Puritan at all. As for 'temperance', though Milton theoretically, no doubt, was all in favour of it, it is not very easy, surely, to read much of his own life in the light of the principle—his own life, or, if it comes to that, his own views. We know that he was no senseless fanatic, but he was a man who habitually took strong lines and who was never deterred, in the processes of his thought, from following what seemed to him to be logic to the most wildly unreasonable of ends. (His discussion of polygamy is a case in point.) And in his general outlook it is rarely a question of finding happy compromises, comfortable and middle ways: it is a question of finding what is right (or what appeals to him as such) and of pursuing this, even to extremes.

But our concern at the moment is with Greenlaw's account of *Paradise Lost* and I would merely make the point that in order to establish his theory of it he has to jettison at least half the text. In his discussion of Adam's fall he leans heavily, as might be expected, on what Milton, through Raphael, tells us we *ought* to think about it; of what Milton has shown us about it (especially in the two key passages discussed) he has literally nothing to say; and his summing up is not much less than a caricature of the truth. Adam fell because he was 'inflamed by a provoking object'; 'the provoking object is not an apple, sign of reasonless and arbitrary prohibition, but *Beauty*'; Adam fell 'through that irrational principle of the soul which operates through lust'.[1] It is strange that the rich text of *Paradise Lost* should ever have yielded such dry and misleading formulae. ('Provoking object' happens to be Milton's own phrase for the apple in the *Areopagitica*; but that hardly justifies Greenlaw's use of it here.) One can only explain such readings by the thought that of all the bad judges of literature, no judge, perhaps, is quite so bad as a good critic in the grip of a preconceived theory. It is

1 Loc. cit. pp. 201, 209, 213.

odd to reflect that Miss Harriet Byron is a safer guide to
Paradise Lost than Greenlaw—than Greenlaw, that is to say,
when bemused by Plato, Aristotle and Spenser.

But the particular point I would make is this: Greenlaw's
theory—that temperance is Milton's theme of themes in
Paradise Lost—is not at all readily applicable to Eve, whatever
may be the case with Adam: so Greenlaw ignores Eve.

Mr Williams does the opposite. Mr Williams, as we have
noted, finds the key to Milton's meaning in 'injured merit'.
Paradise Lost is about the consequences of self-love, about what
happens to people when they let themselves be dominated
by pride, egotism and a sense of their personal rights, forgetting that they are not really 'individual' but 'derived'.
Now 'injured merit' applies perfectly to Satan; with some
forcing it can be made just to touch Eve; but in no way at
all can it apply to Adam. So Mr Williams ignores Adam.
Not absolutely: he gives him five lines, the lines already
quoted (p. 52), in which he makes it clear that he sees a
difficulty in the presentation. (The difficulty of course, is
that Milton has presented Adam as a nearly perfect type
and exemplar of what Mr Williams has just been saying is
the mysterious law and proper order of the universe, self-
abnegation in love.) But he slides by it. The result, however,
is surely a little startling: a theory of *Paradise Lost* that
accounts very well for Satan, provides to some slight extent
for Eve (if we are willing to strain a point or two), but is
obliged to leave Adam completely out in the cold.

And Dr Tillyard, in the end, finds himself caught in
somewhat the same kind of trap. At first he had distinguished
between Adam's gregariousness and Eve's levity. But as he
proceeds the distinction fades. Finally it is dropped, for what
seems to me a quite inadequate reason,[1] and we have the

1 The only reason that Dr Tillyard offers for abandoning his original
distinction is that the last line of the Son's speech ('Was shee thy God',
etc., x, 145) 'seems to show that Milton recognizes a prior cause of
Adam's fall, lack of self-knowledge, itself implying a kind of triviality

summing up: 'I have tried to show that in his treatment of
the Fall Milton meant to condemn the mental levity of Man,
who is prone to forget the importance of his every action....
Feebly they commit what they imagine is a trifling error....' [1]
Is Adam, as he stands there chilled and speechless, an
example of 'mental levity'? Does Adam 'feebly' commit his
error, does he not 'grasp' (Dr Tillyard's word) the significance of what he is about to do? How can such words apply?
This, surely, is maltreatment of the text, and it comes about,
I would suggest, through an over-anxious search for a unifying
principle deeper than Milton's (for his principle is right
under our noses): a principle that will bring all into neat
order and regularity.

I add a few words on the aftermath. It would be profitless
to raise again, I think, the logical difficulties. There was no
way for Milton of making the transition from sinlessness to
sin perfectly intelligible. It is obvious that Adam and Eve
must already have contracted human weaknesses before they
can start on the course of conduct that leads to their fall:
to put it another way, they must already be fallen (technically)
before they can begin to fall. Nor, again, is it possible to see
just how the change from love to lust came about, or what
it was in the act of disobedience that necessitated it. There
is no help for these matters. Mr Lewis, it is true, makes a
heroic effort to draw a distinction between fallen and unfallen
sexuality, and suggests that Dante might have been able to
portray the latter kind successfully. Even Milton, Mr Lewis
thinks, if he had been less explicit—if he had been content to
treat the loves of Adam and Eve 'remotely and mysteriously'

of mind' (op. cit. p. 264). Dr Tillyard refers to the words 'had'st thou
known thy self aright'. But in the first place, as we have noted, this
arraignment of Adam by the Son is based on Adam's self-arraignment,
and that self-arraignment travesties the facts. In the second place, it is
surely of very minor consequence what Milton recognizes or tries to
induce us to recognize as 'a prior cause of Adam's fall'. All that really
matters to us is the cause *as shown*.

1 Op. cit. p. 289.

—might have come near to succeeding. It may be so. It is
perfectly obvious, of course, that nothing would have induced
Milton to rest content with anything of the sort: he was not
that kind of man—or poet. The poet who allowed Adam to
turn the talk so neatly against Raphael with embarrassing
questions about the love-life of angels was not likely to shy
from the task of suggesting the innocent delights of Adam
and Eve. It is perfectly evident, of course, that he very
much enjoyed suggesting them. I cannot help thinking
that Mr Lewis makes an unnecessary to-do about the pro-
vocativeness of Eve's sexual modesty. After the Fall a new
self-consciousness enters, and we have sensuality itself. But
how sensuality could have been absent from prelapsarian
'sex', if prelapsarian 'sex' be granted at all, is rather difficult
to imagine. Milton, at any rate, could not imagine it and
dismissed Augustine's efforts to square this particular circle
(quite rightly) as nonsense.

Milton's triumph in what follows is, of course, the delineation of Eve. It is like watching some magic transformation;
the Fall transmutes her into a woman, a person; one by one
the human lineaments are etched in before our eyes. She
has not spoken a dozen lines before she is there, alive:

> other care perhaps
> May have diverted from continual watch
> Our great Forbidder, safe with all his Spies
> About him.   (ix, 813)

Already, as Professor Stoll puts it, she is showing a 'defensive
reaction',[1] dramatizing herself as in some obscure way
injured: it makes her feel less guilty to reproach God, to
suggest that it is all, in some indefinable sense, His fault.
Do not let us be too hard on her for the jealous spasm that
follows:

> but what if God have seen
> And Death ensue? then I shall be no more,
> And *Adam* wedded to another *Eve*,

1 *Poets and Playwrights* (1930), p. 261.

> Shall live with her enjoying, I extinct;
> A death to think. Confirm'd then I resolve,
> *Adam* shall share with me in bliss or woe:
> So dear I love him, that with him all deaths
> I could endure, without him live no life.   (IX, 826)

This, says Mr Lewis, is Murder. In a sense perhaps it is; and in a not dissimilar sense each of us commits murder five times a week; but we should not like to be called murderers. It is not as if she knew what death exactly was; nor is it quite fair, if we are to come down with a heavy hand on her jealous and possessive impulse here, to ignore (as Mr Lewis does) those other impulses—of love, heroism, self-sacrifice—that she shows in so many a later passage. Indeed we have only to move on forty lines to find one:

> Thou therefore also taste, that equal Lot
> May joyne us, equal Joy, as equal Love;
> Least thou not tasting, different degree
> Disjoyne us, and I then too late renounce
> Deitie for thee, when Fate will not permit.   (IX, 881)

She means this, and who does not feel that she would be capable of it, that if Adam were to be left she would tear herself away from deity, if she could, to go back to him! She fibs sometimes. Carried away by Adam's loyalty, which so enhances her own value, she says:

> Were it I thought Death menac't would ensue
> This my attempt, I would sustain alone
> The worst, and not perswade thee, rather die
> Deserted.   (IX, 977)

She is a liar, but who cares? She has found the right 'objective correlative' for her feelings.

The picture of the 'distemper' of Adam and Eve is itself a minor masterpiece, all the better for the glint of sardonic humour that Milton allows to intrude. Adam eats and is enraptured:

> if such pleasure be
> In things to us forbidden, it might be wish'd,
> For this one Tree had bin forbidden ten.   (IX, 1024)

'We can hear Eve's hectic, infatuate giggles at Adam's words', says Dr Tillyard; and so we can.

From now on, indeed, as far as Eve is concerned, Milton's bonds are fairly untied. The problem was somewhat different with Adam. He must remain stilted. He has so much still to exemplify, so much of the burden of the doctrine still to carry, that he can never win through to complete freedom as a man. But Eve's humanity only deepens as the poem moves towards its end. In the debates in Book x hers are the words that reach our hearts:

> While yet we live, scarse one short hour perhaps,
> Between us two let there be peace, both joyning. (x, 924)

And again:

> both have sin'd, but thou
> Against God onely, I against God and thee,
> And to the place of judgement will return,
> There with my cries importune Heaven, that all
> The sentence from thy head remov'd may light
> On me, sole cause to thee of all this woe,
> Mee mee onely just object of his ire. (x, 930)

Impetuous though the offer is, she is not pretending, and Adam, though he makes what she has said the text for another little lecture, scolds gently. On their joint problems she brings her realistic, ruthless woman's sense to bear. If the future of their 'descent' is what chiefly perplexes, then she advises: let there be no 'descent', prevent the race unblest. If that involves too hard an abstention, then she suggests the suicide pact. Both are eminently practical, drastic, knot-cutting proposals. Again she receives a slight scolding. But to our minds she has the better of it, and it is pleasant that the last words spoken in the poem should be hers. She regrets Eden, but Adam, after all, is her world. She links arms with him and faces the future.

CHAPTER IV

SATAN AND THE TECHNIQUE OF DEGRADATION

If the drift of the preceding chapters has any rightness it would follow that some of the major difficulties that we now find in *Paradise Lost* are due, quite simply, to Milton's inexperience in the assessment of narrative problems. It is not, I think, mere folly or presumption to suggest that this is so. Narrative is a special art, and the greatest of poets may not be capable of apprehending instinctively the traps and danger-spots of an especially intricate and difficult theme. There were besides, as we have noted, reasons inherent in the very nature of this theme why Milton was not in a position to appreciate its full complexity. But, inexperienced or not, and unable, as he may have been, to estimate the true explosive qualities of his material, he knew one thing: he had to be interesting. That was the paramount necessity; and it was a necessity that immediately set certain conditions for the delineation of Satan and his fellows.

It was essential, in the first place, that the rebellion should seem credible; and this meant, in turn, that there had to be some uncertainty, or at least some *illusion* of uncertainty, about the facts. It will be remembered that Milton makes his initial statement in carefully generalized terms: the really awkward details come much later, where they will do less harm. At the opening of the poem we hear merely that Satan made a great bid for supremacy and that his motive was pride; the exact occasion of the revolt is left, for the time being, obscure. Again, it is not until we are two-thirds of the way through Book II that we learn what the

odds against the rebels were: two to one. We hear this from
Death:

> Art thou that Traitor Angel, art thou he,
> Who first broke peace in Heav'n and Faith, till then
> Unbrok'n, and in proud rebellious Arms
> Drew after him the third part of Heav'ns Sons...?
>
> (II, 689)

By this time Satan has become in our imaginations so for-
midable a figure that we take the news in our stride; in any
case it is slipped in so unemphatically that we receive it
almost without thinking about it. To have given it earlier
and at all pointedly would have been to cast doubt on the
quality of Satan's brain. The impression, carefully built up
in Book I and confirmed in Book II, is that the rebellion (in
the eyes, of course, of the rebels) was a thoroughly rational
undertaking, with a fair fighting chance of success. The
qualification 'in the eyes of the rebels' is not fatuous: the
rebels have to be allowed their estimate. God, the event has
now shown, was the stronger; but, as Satan says:

> till then who knew
> The force of those dire Arms? (I, 93)

The conclusion must now be accepted, says Beëlzebub, that
God *is* almighty,

> since no less
> Then such could hav orepow'rd such force as ours.
>
> (I, 144)

We should not gather from this line, and are not meant to,
that their party was outnumbered two to one; nor should
we have gathered it from Satan's words a little earlier about
'innumerable force of Spirits arm'd'. Indeed, the tone of all
the discussion is to keep that fact well out of sight. The rebels
shook the throne of God, says Satan, and made him doubt
his empire. They endangered Heaven's perpetual King, says
Beëlzebub,

> And put to proof his high Supremacy,
> Whether upheld by strength, or Chance, or Fate. (I, 132)

Up till then, says Satan, God had occupied his throne 'secure',

> but still his strength conceal'd,
> Which tempted our attempt, and wrought our fall. (1, 641)

As we read through Books I and II we do not check at such lines and remind ourselves that Satan is a liar, nor does Milton expect us to do so. We feel the element of bravado in the language; we know that in such circumstances we cannot look for strict accuracy; we do not take the words of these defeated ones for a perfectly literal report of fact. But the drift of their talk cannot but affect us, and it is meant to affect us. Mr Williams (interested throughout in his key principles of 'derivation' and 'self-love') seems to me to miss completely the narrative impressions that Milton is striving after in these books. 'Milton', he says, 'knew as well as we do that Omnipotence cannot be shaken.'[1] Certainly he did; and for that very reason he must do his best as a narrative poet (it was elementary technique) to make us forget the fact, must try by every craft of narrative at his command to instil into us the temporary illusion that Omnipotence *can* be shaken —until such time, at least, as he has his poem properly moving and Satan securely established in our imaginations as a worthy Antagonist of Heaven. The rebellion, we know well, was 'a foolish effort': we know it if we stop to think. But if the net effect of Milton's writing in Book I had been to make us *feel* that it was mere foolishness he might just as well have laid aside his work there and then. 'Much of *Paradise Lost* can be felt to revolve, laughingly and harmoniously, round the solemn and helpless image of pride.'[2] Much of it may; it is quite certain that the great opening books of the poem do not; Milton's chief care has been precisely to see to it that they do not.

Actually, if the text is watched closely it will be seen, I think, that there is a certain equivocation in the use of the

[1] Loc. cit. p. xv.   [2] Ibid p. x.

word 'omnipotent'. When it is convenient to do so Milton uses it with full literal force; but on occasion it can seem not much more than a grandiloquent synonym for 'supreme'. There is a certain latitude or 'play' in the use of the word; and this for the benefit of the narrative. Similarly, we do not quite know, in reading the first and second books, whether we are to accept as absolutely fixed and definite facts the immortality of the fallen angels and the eternity of their doom. We are pretty sure, of course, where the truth lies. All the same, the questions are kept slightly controversial; and this, again, is for the good of the narrative. The grain of doubt left by such lines as

> Or if our substance be indeed Divine
> And cannot cease to be, (II, 99)

or

> Suppose he should relent
> And publish Grace to all, on promise made
> Of new Subjection, (II, 237)

small though it is, helps to make the situation of the rebels interesting and enhances their dignity in debate.

It is much the same with Satan's own inconsistencies. 'Hell is inaccurate', says Mr Williams. So, it may be remarked, is Heaven, if we may take the Son's account of the Fall of Man (already noted) as a fair sample of heavenly accuracy. But it seems obvious that the inaccuracies of Satan are sometimes rhetorical rather than real (inaccuracies of expression rather than of thought), and that when they are real they are often being used as deliberate debating points. A clear example of the first kind is his speech from the throne at the beginning of Book II. Mr Lewis cites it as one of two passages that prove that Satan is already wilting under the doom of Nonsense—that his brain is already in process of decay.

> Powers and Dominions, Deities of Heav'n,
> For since no deep within her gulf can hold
> Immortal vigor, though opprest and fall'n

I give not Heav'n for lost. From this descent
Celestial vertues rising, will appear
More glorious and more dread then from no fall
And trust themselves to fear no second fate:
Mee though just right, and the fixt Laws of Heav'n
Did first create your Leader, next, free choice,
With what besides, in Counsel or in Fight,
Hath bin achievd of merit, yet this loss
Thus farr at least recover'd, hath much more
Establisht in a safe unenvied Throne
Yielded with full consent. The happier state
In Heav'n, which follows dignity, might draw
Envy from each inferior; but who here
Will envy whom the highest place exposes
Formost to stand against the Thunderers aime
Your bulwark, and condemns to greatest share
Of endless pain? where there is then no good
For which to strive, no strife can grow up there
From Faction; for none sure will claim in hell
Precedence, none, whose portion is so small
Of present pain, that with ambitious mind
Will covet more. With this advantage then
To union, and firm Faith, and firm accord,
More then can be in Heav'n, we now return
To claim our just inheritance of old,
Surer to prosper then prosperity
Could have assur'd us; and by what best way,
Whether of open Warr or covert guile,
We now debate; who can advise, may speak.   (II, 11)

Of course there are contradictions in the speech, as there
are in a good epigram or a string of humorous and effective
paradoxes. The argument, indeed, is deliberately tinged with
paradox: it has, in such ways, a nicely calculated appeal.
'Safe unenvied Throne', 'none sure will claim in hell Precedence': these sallies deserved, and perhaps (we may imagine)
got, the faintest stir of amused response. The wry ironic note
is exactly suited to the occasion; and the more direct implications of 'condemns to greatest share Of endless pain' would
have gone home. When a mother picks up a hurt child and
brings a bleak smile by some quickly improvised comfort we
do not examine what she says for 'logic': we judge it by its

effect. So here. The logic of the speech, naturally, is insecure. His throne is safe and unenvied, argues Satan, because the misery of the rebels is complete; it follows that every improvement in their state must tend to weaken his authority (since misery is its basis) and to sap the firmness of their union; yet the firmness of their union is the very ground he gives for his hope of victory. This (as Mr Lewis points out) is what the argument means if it is looked into. But it is not meant to be looked into—it is not that kind of argument; nor, because of these latent absurdities, is it justifiably branded as nonsense. On the contrary, it is exceedingly good sense, of the sort that Satan requires for the moment's ends. The whole aim of the speech, obviously, is to instil a mood, to cheer spirits, to confirm a confederacy that after the shocks it has just been receiving might easily be on the verge of total collapse. If his spurious impromptu reasoning accomplishes those immediate results it will have served the sole use it was meant for. In short it is the kind of speech that able commanders, one supposes, have been making at such critical junctures since the dawn of history. The specious logic betrays, of course, the desperateness of the situation. Nevertheless, to appraise such a speech by logic alone is to bring under the same ban of Nonsense, by implication, half the great oratory of the world.

Satan's other 'nonsensical' speech occurs in Book v. It is his reply to Abdiel, who alone opposed the 'current of his fury'.

> That we were formd then saist thou? & the work
> Of secondarie hands, by task transferd
> From Father to his Son? strange point and new!
> Doctrin which we would know whence learnt: who saw
> When this creation was? rememberst thou
> Thy making, while the Maker gave thee being?
> We know no time when we were not as now;
> Know none before us, self-begot, self-rais'd
> By our own quick'ning power, when fatal course
> Had circl'd his full Orbe, the birth mature

> Of this our native Heav'n, Ethereal Sons.
> Our puissance is our own, our own right hand
> Shall teach us highest deeds, by proof to try
> Who is our equal: then thou shalt behold
> Whether by supplication we intend
> Address, and to begirt th' Almighty Throne
> Beseeching or besieging. This report,
> These tidings carrie to th' anointed King;
> And fly, ere evil intercept thy flight.   (v, 850)

It must be admitted that in the wordy warfare Satan is hard pressed. In Books v and vi Milton allows the truth of things to come more into the open, and Abdiel more than once gets well inside Satan's guard. Abdiel (as Milton's mouthpiece) has just delivered the 'official' view on the creation of angels. The angels, he informs the assembly, were created by the Son himself, acting as the Word. This is a heavy thrust, and even though none 'seconds' Abdiel Satan must say something. He makes two not ineffective rejoinders: first, that the point is new; and second, that Abdiel's account of the creation of himself and other angels must necessarily be based on hearsay. Neither rejoinder is silly. The point *must* be new, or he could not in full assembly say it was. We are not told why it is that Abdiel is so exceptionally well informed; for some reason he is, just as for some reason the rebel angels appear to have been kept in the dark about a number of other facts that good angels know. However that may be, Satan is at a disadvantage and must improvise. I do not think it can be said that he improvises nonsensically. Even the notion of the 'self-begetting' is good enough to serve as an argumentative stop-gap, and that is all that Satan wants it for. Whether this particular thought had ever occurred to him before or ever occurred to him again we naturally do not know; it has all the air of a 'bright idea' caught on the wing. But surely nothing of this tells—or is meant by Milton to tell—very seriously against Satan's intellect. He is making the best show he can and is not undeserving, on debating points, of the 'hoarce murmur' that presently 'echo'd to his words applause'.

Nor, finally, does Milton allow the motive for the revolt which (generalized previously) he now takes occasion to explain in more detail, to impress us as merely fantastic. That, again, would be to spoil Satan too soon, spoil therefore the story, spoil the poem. The motive, actually, would seem to have been made rather more plausible than Milton intended, for God's announcement of the exaltation of the Son has, in plain fact, a distinctly curt and challenging air. Abdiel, again as Milton's spokesman, avers that it was never in God's mind to offer a slight, for

> by experience taught we know how good,
> And of our good, and of our dignitie
> How provident he is, how farr from thought
> To make us less, bent rather to exalt
> Our happie state under one Head more neer
> United.   (v, 823)

The real effect of the appointment, he adds, will be to elevate rather than to depress the status of the angelic host:

> since he the Head
> One of our number thus reduc't becomes.   (v, 839)

It is ingenious, and we understand well that we are to accept this as the official view; but it is not exactly what God said, and it is most decidedly not how God sounded, when he made the declaration of appointment. We cannot with any reasonableness talk of Satan's 'wrongs'. In theory, at least, there are no wrongs, and we know so little about the facts of the matter that we are not in a position to dispute the theory. The background of Satan's revolt is, so to say, non-existent: we cannot argue from it, because it is not there. If we began to think about it at all deeply we should be obliged, no doubt, to agree with Sir Herbert Grierson that 'if the third part of a school or college or nation broke into rebellion we should be driven, or strongly disposed, to suspect some mismanagement by the supreme powers'.[1] The alternative, he suggests, would be to 'attribute to the rebels a double dose of original sin'; which in the case of the angelic rebels, at least, would again raise awkward questions, seeing that original sin had not yet been invented. There is no use at all, of course, in probing behind what we are given: we can only take the narrative as we find it; and when we respond naturally, Satan's sense of having been passed over, of having suffered impairment through the appointment of the Son, certainly does not affect us (as Mr Lewis and Mr Williams think it should) as laughable. 'In the midst of a world of light and love, of song and feast and dance, he could find nothing to think of more interesting than his own prestige.'[2] If this had been exactly the impression of the poem, Satan's offended pride perhaps *would* have been nothing less than ridiculous. (Think, for example, of the effect of a jealous Satan planted in the middle of the *Paradiso*.) But it is not exactly the impression of the poem. There is no sign of love in God's speech of appointment. On the contrary, the speech is dictatorial and full of threats:

> him who disobeyes
> Mee disobeyes, breaks union, and that day
> Cast out from God and blessed vision, falls
> Into utter darkness, deep ingulft, his place
> Ordaind without redemption, without end.   (v, 611)

And to repeat, God pays nobody the compliment (unless it be Abdiel) of explaining just why he is taking this momentous step.

Milton's problem, in truth, was very difficult. He must give Satan a reason for revolting, a reason that does not put him outside the pale of our interest—make him merely absurd. But it must still be a bad reason: the revolt must still be strange, unpardonable, abhorrent. The truth surely is that

1 *Milton and Wordsworth* (1937), p. 116.
2 C. S. Lewis, op. cit. p. 94.

Milton succeeded in suggesting a rather greater degree of provocation for it, and therefore of reasonableness in it, than he ever intended.

Let us return for a little to the Satan of the first two books. There are really no problems for *us* in the Satan of these books: the problems were all for Milton; and the chief risk he had to face seems obvious. Given a writer of even rudimentary narrative instincts there was not much doubt that Satan would be impressive: the danger, of course, was that his impressiveness could so easily get out of control. But there is no puzzle in this, surely; nothing that needs intricate accounting for. Mr Lewis goes deep to explain the primacy of Satan as a character. His theory, briefly, is that a 'bad' character is always easier to draw than a 'good' one, for 'to make a character worse than oneself it is only necessary to release imaginatively from control some of the bad passions which, in real life, are always straining at the leash; the Satan, the Iago, the Becky Sharp, within each of us, is always there and only too ready, the moment the leash is slipped, to come out and have in our books that holiday we try to deny them in our lives'.[1] To draw a 'bad' character, in short, it is only necessary to relax, be oneself; to draw a 'good' one it is necessary to rise above oneself; hence the scarcity of well drawn 'good' characters, the abundance of well drawn 'bad'. If we needed a theory to account for the pre-eminence of Satan among the characters of *Paradise Lost* this theory would certainly suffice. But the more one ponders the theory (which takes its rise in some basic principles of Mr Lewis's moral thinking) the more one doubts its validity. Numerous examples would appear to tell against it. And what exactly is meant by 'good'? When we talk of drawing a good character we do not usually mean drawing a saint. The character of a saint is perhaps difficult to draw, for at least it takes us

1 Op. cit. p. 98.

into a limiting (in a sense into a freakish) region of human experience. And does not that rather suggest what the real fact may be? Is there not a central range of character and is it not perhaps true that the farther we move out towards *either* extreme, the 'good' or the 'bad', the harder becomes the task?

But whatever the validity of Mr Lewis's theory in general, the application of it to Satan seems quite superfluous. We need none of Mr Lewis's reasons to see why it is that Satan *must* stand out from the other characters of *Paradise Lost*. It is because he is the only character in the story whom in any real sense it was possible to draw at all. 'Set a hundred poets to tell the same story,' says Mr Lewis, 'and in ninety of the resulting poems Satan will be the best character.'[1] Exactly; or not quite exactly, for Mr Lewis's figures are inaccurate: in a *hundred* of the resulting poems (supposing the writers to have even an elementary appreciation of the narrative possibilities of their material) Satan will be the best character. For, to repeat, the simple fact is that he has not, and in such circumstances could not have, any competition whatever.

But quite apart from the inherent conditions of the theme— conditions that almost force him into pre-eminence—Satan, we understand well, was a predestined character for Milton. There need, surely, be no confusion here, no perplexity about the 'sympathy', conscious or unconscious, that Milton felt for his creation. Of course it does not mean that Milton, as we ordinarily use the phrase, was on Satan's side. It means merely that he was able, in a marked degree, to conceive Satan in terms of himself: in terms of the temptations to which he felt his own nature especially liable, and of the values, too, to which his own nature especially responded. I say 'to a marked degree', because there is nothing exclusive in Milton's sympathy with Satan. Milton seems to us often, as he writes of him, to be giving of his own substance, but he can give of his own substance anywhere. In those alter-

1 Op. cit. p. 98.

cations, for example, between Satan and Abdiel in Books v and vi we *feel* Milton now in the lines of the one, now in the lines of the other, but chiefly, without any doubt, in the lines of Abdiel. In the concluding paragraph of Book v the sympathy is so close that there is virtually an identification: in speaking of Abdiel Milton might (as so many have noted) be speaking of himself: the lines come to us with the weight of some of the intensest memories of his life behind them.

There is, I think, a further distinction to be made. Mr Bernard Shaw once remarked that it is the habit of a sentimentalist to assume that human qualities come in neatly assorted sets, that they are 'matched' in people's natures like colours. In life, as he pointed out, such harmonious assortments of matched qualities are not so frequently found: a war hero may be spiteful and may turn out to be an unexpectedly bad loser at games; a lovable woman may be greedy, untrustworthy in financial affairs, and not a strict speaker of the truth; and so on. And just as we have to admit that lying and spitefulness are reprehensible (even though consisting in the same nature with charm and heroism) so we have to admit that courage in a gangster is still courage and therefore good. Now when Mr Lewis writes of Satan he writes for the moment, I think, as a sentimentalist. He wishes to see Satan's character as made up of aesthetically harmonious qualities—of qualities that match. He is reluctant to admit that we can condemn Satan for some things and at the same time find him extremely admirable for others. So he compiles for him a little list of traits that agree—a list, I think, that quite falsifies the impressions yielded by the first two books. We have in Satan, he says, an expression of Milton's 'own pride, malice, folly, misery, and lust'.[1] But Milton expresses in Satan much more of himself than this, and such a picture of the Satan of the

1 Op. cit. p. 99.

first two books is surely a very partial portrait. We hear about Satan's pride, see something of it, and have no difficulty in believing in it; the lust is tossed in gratuitously—I doubt if we ever really believe in it: there is no particular reason why we should;[1] we see something of his malice, we can perhaps deduce his folly, and we know that theoretically he and his mates are in misery. But what we are chiefly made to see and feel in the first two books are quite different things: fortitude in adversity, enormous endurance, a certain splendid recklessness, remarkable powers of rising to an occasion, extraordinary qualities of leadership (shown not least in his salutary taunts), and striking intelligence in meeting difficulties that are novel and could seem overwhelming. What we feel most of all, I suppose, is his refusal to give in—just that. How can Milton help sympathizing with qualities such as these? Obviously he sympathizes with them. In this sense and to this extent he *is* on Satan's side, as it was quite proper for him to be.

So far the situation seems very clear. But it is evident that portraiture so sympathetic, drawing such strength from Milton's own life and nature, could be very dangerous for Milton's scheme. Of course it was dangerous; and nothing is more interesting, technically, in the opening books than to note the nervousness that creeps on Milton as he becomes aware of what is threatening. It is an instructive and in some ways an amusing study. If one observes what is happening one sees that there is hardly a great speech of Satan's that

1 Why we should believe in it, that is to say, in the sense in which we believe in his pride or his courage or his arrogance. In this respect the lust of Satan is not unlike the 'luxury' of Macbeth, which is also something *declared*, something extraneous, properly, to the portrait: take it away and the portrait is just the same. Take away Satan's lust and the portrait is just the same, for no matter what Milton may have had at the back of his mind in introducing it, artistically it is an extra. To say with M. Saurat that Satan represents 'in particular' sensuality seems to me absurd: absurd, indeed, in precisely the same way as it would be to say that Macbeth stands especially for viciousness and loose living.

Milton is not at pains to correct, to damp down and neutralize. He will put some glorious thing in Satan's mouth, then, anxious about the effect of it, will pull us gently by the sleeve, saying (for this is what it amounts to): 'Do not be carried away by this fellow: he *sounds* splendid, but take my word for it. . . .' We have in fact, once again, the two levels: the level of demonstration or exhibition, and the level of allegation or commentary; and again there is disagreement. What is conveyed on the one level is for a large part of the time not in accord with what is conveyed on the other. Milton's allegations *clash* with his demonstrations.

The process begins, indeed, quite early in the poem. After Satan's very first speech comes the comment:

> So spake th' Apostate Angel, though in pain,
> Vaunting aloud, but rackt with deep despare.   (1, 125)

Has there been much despair in what we have just been listening to? The speech would almost seem to be incompatible with that. To accept Milton's comment here (as most readers appear to do) as if it had a validity equal to that of the speech itself is surely very naïve critical procedure. I emphasize the point again, because here too it becomes of the first importance for our estimate of what is happening in the poem—for our view, in fact, of what the poem actually *is*: in any work of imaginative literature at all it is the demonstration, by the very nature of the case, that has the higher validity: an allegation can possess no comparable authority. Of course they should agree; but if they do not then the demonstration must carry the day. In the present passage, had Milton very much in mind, one wonders, when he penned his comment? Did he really feel, when he wrote the words, that Satan *was* in 'deep despare'? It seems to me that if he had felt the despair he simply could not have written the speech as it is. Surely the truth is obvious that the phrase is half mechanical: it is the first of a long line of automatic snubs, of perfunctory jabs and growls. Each great speech lifts Satan a little beyond what Milton really intended, so he suppresses him again (or tries to) in a comment.

The procedure has been noted by other critics (though not as a rule, I think, from quite this point of view) and could be illustrated at length. There are the guarding phrases a little later:

> but he his wonted pride
> Soon recollecting, with high words, that bore
> *Semblance of worth not substance*, gently rais'd
> Their fainted courage, and dispel'd their fears.   (i, 527)

In a similar way the speech of Belial in Book ii receives its prompt corrective. Belial's speech, as I suppose nearly all readers of the poem feel when they are left to themselves, is one of the most notable of those delivered in the infernal conclave; it is not only eloquent and poetically impressive: it is impregnated with strong common sense. And Belial, besides, counsels what Milton theoretically ought to approve —peace. His advice to his fellows is to stay where they are, to be quiet and unprovocative, to lie low and wait and see. In the circumstances, especially as we know from other sources that they have no hope of grace, it is difficult to see what better advice could have been given. But Milton dislikes Belial. To 'low thoughts' of this sort he much prefers (although he will not say so) dashing villainy. So Belial is snubbed.

> Thus *Belial* with words cloath'd in reasons garb
> Counsel'd ignoble ease, and peaceful sloath,
> Not peace.   (ii, 226)

Belial's words are not only 'cloath'd in reasons garb': they *are* reasonable. The ease he counsels may be ignoble, but it would have been interesting to hear what kind of activity Milton could have recommended in place of it, seeing that theoretically the bad angels are in hell to stay. And the distinction between 'peaceful sloath' and 'peace' is very much of the nature of a quibble. Milton's perfectly brazen object, in short, is to discredit Belial. What he gives with one hand he takes away with the other. Having permitted his character to speak well and wisely he then says that he has spoken meanly and foolishly. What he has just affirmed (through a demonstration) he now denies (in a comment).

The method, though entertaining, is a little unfair to the characters concerned, and so are the other devices that Milton uses to the same end. After Beëlzebub has spoken we have this:

> Thus *Beëlzebub*
> Pleaded his devilish Counsel, first devis'd
> By *Satan*, and in part propos'd: for whence,
> But from the Author of all ill could Spring
> So deep a malice, to confound the race
> Of mankind in one root, and Earth with Hell
> To mingle and involve, done all to spite
> The great Creatour? (ii, 378)

Satan, of course, threw out a suggestion in Book i that the rebels might try their luck against the rumoured new world, or tackle Heaven on some other flank. His main point was that they should make an eruption *somewhere* as soon as possible, and resume the attack.

A few lines farther on we have this (Satan has just accepted the perilous scouting mission to the new world):

> Thus saying rose
> The Monarch, and prevented all reply,
> Prudent, least from his resolution rais'd
> Others among the chief might offer now
> (Certain to be refus'd) what erst they feard;
> And so refus'd might in opinion stand
> His rivals, winning cheap the high repute
> Which he through hazard huge must earn. (ii, 466)

The neutralizing intent is again very clear. Satan has just done, when all is said, a noble thing, but it would be inconvenient to leave that impression untarnished. So Milton proceeds to tarnish it by impressing over it the image of Satan as astute politician.

The technique, indeed, is almost comically transparent and in its nature (we may fairly say) is rather primitive. Using the method of allegation Milton can produce a trump card whenever he wishes. We have no defence against such tactics except, of course, to take due note of what is going on and to decline to play when the trump has appeared too obviously from Milton's sleeve. The most flagrant example of this kind of literary cheating occurs, I think, in Book IV. Gabriel, who has not been markedly successful in debate, retorts on the Adversary:

> And thou sly hypocrite, who now wouldst seem
> Patron of liberty, who more then thou
> Once fawn'd, and cring'd, and servilly ador'd
> Heav'ns awful Monarch? (IV, 957)

Are we, then, on Gabriel's undocumented assertion, to make an effort to accommodate the Satan we know to a Satan who 'once fawn'd, and cring'd, and servilly ador'd'? Why should we accept this high-handed piece of unsupported calumny? This seems beyond reasonable bounds, this is not keeping to the rules of the game at all.

But in the first two books of the poem such measures are really signs of nervousness and do not affect appreciably the single tremendous impression that Satan (rather in excess of Milton's will) has made. Everybody feels that the Satan of the first two books stands alone; after them comes a break, and he is never as impressive again. If we leave aside the unimportant 'accosting' of Uriel towards the end of Book III we hear him next in the famous 'address to the Sun' (IV, 32) in which he 'falls into many doubts with himself, and many passions, fear, envy, and despare'.

I do not think that it is possible to overestimate the effect of this break. Its significance, I think, is much greater than is usually admitted. It is in every respect, I would suggest, an interruption. It is not merely that the Satan of the first two books re-enters altered: the Satan of the first two books to all intents and purposes *disappears*: I do not think that in any true sense we ever see him again.

Milton's task in this, the second part of the delineation, is of course to trace the development of Satan. Now a character in process of change may affect us in either of two ways. If we have been given the requisite clues the development will seem, as it were, to carry its own guarantees with it. It is so with Macbeth. The preliminary glimpses we have of his nature, few and partial though they may seem to be, are enough; because of them we do not question the curiously unexpected turns his development takes. We could hardly have predicted those turns, but when they come we know that they are the right ones. It is as if the progress is self-proving; the keys with which we have been furnished fit; our feelings give us assurance that the man we saw could and would, in the given conditions, change into the man we see. And the progress of Lady Macbeth (so different in its course) is exactly the same in kind.

The progress of Satan is utterly distinct in its nature, and it seems to me that unless we recognize this we are not seeing the poem aright. The extreme simplification of the method in Books i and ii leaves us with a memorable, indeed an overpowering, image: but the image is self-complete, finished. To expect it to develop is like expecting a statue of Michelangelo's to develop. We make, surely, a new start. The Satan of the address to the Sun is not a development from the old, he is not a changed Satan, he is a *new* Satan. We can make the transition from the one to the other, I think, in only one way: by spinning a bridge of theory across and above the visible presentment. A doctrine—that Pride, say, has certain consequences—will carry us across: I would suggest that we cannot make the crossing imaginatively. What it comes to is that we are obliged to take this new Satan, and, indeed, all the steps of this new Satan's subsequent history, on trust.

I do not think, in other words, that the term 'degeneration', applied to the downward course of Satan, has any real validity. Macbeth degenerates—in some respects, at least. A character in a piece of imaginative literature degenerates when we are in a position to check his progress by what we know of him: when we are made to feel that this or that change, once we are shown it, does follow, although we ourselves could not, perhaps, have foretold it. But what we have in the alleged 'degeneration' of Satan is really, on a large scale and in a disguised form, what we have had in the running fire of belittling commentary already noted. It is a pretended exhibition of changes occurring; actually it is of the nature of an assertion that certain changes occur. The changes do not generate themselves from within: they are imposed from without. Satan, in short, does not degenerate: *he is degraded*.

It is not surprising, therefore, that this second part of the presentation of Satan should come, increasingly, to be marked by devices that had no place in the first. In particular one might, perhaps, have predicted that the general weakness of the method would betray itself (as in fact it does) in one special way: in the steady drift towards allegory.

Let us, at all events, review rapidly in the light of this reading the main stages in Satan's downward course. We begin with the soliloquy near the opening of Book IV. It is a speech, of course, utterly different in feeling and texture from any speech that has preceded it. As a piece of writing, indeed, it probably strikes every sensitive reader (whether he has heard of Phillips or not) as a little odd in *Paradise Lost*. There is a reason, as we know, for the oddity. Phillips tells us that the soliloquy had been designed by Milton as the opening speech of a tragedy, and that some lines of it were in writing several years before the poem was begun. It is natural, therefore, that it should have the 'feel' of an extended Elizabethan soliloquy, and numerous resemblances have been noted. Perhaps the most interesting is the likeness in some lines to the prayer of Claudius.[1] The Satan of this speech is another 'limed soul':

> O then at last relent: is there no place
> Left for Repentance, none for Pardon left?
> None left but by submission; and that word
> *Disdain* forbids me. (IV, 79)

The speech, then, was conceived and in part, at least, composed before Milton began his poem. What is the conclusion? Mr Lewis sees in the fact a clear warning that we must not read any *accidental* quality into the progress of Satan. It is not as if Milton, having blundered in the earlier books by making Satan much more glorious than he ever meant to do, had sought then somewhat belatedly to rectify his errors. I think we may easily accept this, and yet feel that it is not quite fair to the total impression to say that Milton in the first two books is occupied merely in putting 'the most specious aspects of Satan' in their proper place, at the beginning of the poem: letting Satan have his head, so to say, at the outset, giving him a run for his money; the implication being that while all this is going on Milton has his mind firmly fixed on the goal towards which everything is moving, the important soliloquy of doubt and self-torture already conceived.

Do creative artists work in quite this way? In a sense, no doubt, the soliloquy was the conception from which Milton started: in the sense that he had already thought of it and in parts written it. But surely nothing is more evident than that when Milton changed over from his tragedy to his epic the whole equilibrium of what he was about to do suffered a shift. It was hardly any longer a question of the old soliloquy controlling the new work: the question was rather whether it could find a quite satisfactory niche in the new

---

1 Hanford pointed out the resemblance (*Studies in Philology*, 1917, p. 190) thinking that it had not been noticed previously. But Newton had observed it.

context at all, whether, as it stood, it was usable. As it turned out it was usable; but the difference of texture is enough to cause a slight feeling of strangeness, and I do not think any reader can escape a sense of abruptness in the placing.

The abruptness seems to me everything. In the projected tragedy this magnificent soliloquy would have borne on us with its full weight, would have made a direct, unhindered impact. It would have put a stamp on the work that nothing thereafter could have erased. Everything that followed would necessarily have been referred back to it. It would have given us our dominant lead, would have decided, in the first few minutes, what our characteristic attitude to Satan was to be. Milton designed the soliloquy, wrote part of it and put it away. Then, still keeping it by him for use, he began his epic. But now our key, our centre, is quite different; and just as in the other case it would have been impossible to nullify, or even very much to modify, that opening all-powerful impression, so here in the epic the cue is given past alteration: the Satan of the first two books is established once and for all and nothing will avail against him.[1]

1 Mr Musgrove ('Is the Devil an Ass?', *The Review of English Studies*, October 1945, p. 302) makes the point that we start the poem with certain presumptions about Satan, and that these presumptions give us the power to override to a considerable extent the impression that Satan makes in the first two books. We know that the 'real' Satan will come on the scene in due course; our business in the meantime is not to take the first Satan too seriously.

I think that Mr Musgrove tends to exaggerate the place and importance of presumptions in literature. It is obvious that we start any book about any well-known character, from Joseph to Joan of Arc and beyond, with presumptions; we start *Paradise Lost* itself with some fairly strong presumptions about God. But a great deal of the interest of reading consists in the process—which starts automatically—of checking the presumptions we have brought with us against the impressions we receive; and if we hang back and fight against the impressions—as it seems to me Mr Musgrove does—we at least run the risk of robbing ourselves of a great deal of the interest of reading new books about well-known people.

Mr Musgrove cites the authority of Horace. But Horace, strictly speaking, had nothing to say to *readers* on this score: in his dictum about

For it is too much to ask of us, at the beginning of Book IV, that we should come to terms, unwarned, unprepared, with this sudden new Satan who finds, when on the brink of his attempt, that he has brought Hell with him in his breast. Why? What faintest signs were there that anything like this could happen? What filaments, however tenuous, stretch back from this speech of horror and uncertainty and trouble to the Satan of the first books? The soliloquy is a masterpiece, and yet it is to it, properly speaking, that the 'speciousness' belongs. It is specious in its context because the Satan who now begins to unsay all that the other Satan said, who all of a sudden recognizes his 'Pride and worse Ambition' for what they are, who is softened by remorse ('Ah wherefore! he deserv'd no such return'), who realizes belatedly that the service of God was not hard at all, who knows now that he himself is Hell, who lectures perspicuously on his helpless case and example—this is a Satan that we have not felt before, not even dimly felt. And now that he is put before us we still cannot see the connection.

What follows has really, then, nothing to do with 'character'. Perhaps Satan never was a 'character' in the full sense of the word: a tremendous emblem, rather, giving the illusion, through two tremendous books, of life. I do not think he gives that illusion any longer. *Why* does Satan deteriorate? Milton could not say, for 'pride' is no sufficient answer. The whole process is abstract. The point, of course, is that we do not, and in the peculiar circumstances cannot, know the roots of anything, for it was never possible to endow Satan in any

'following report' he was addressing writers; and it is by no means certain that he would have approved of Milton's procedures. So many powerful and unmistakable *departures* from the traditional reports of Satan—so early in the poem—might well have struck him as unwise in the extreme (as in a sense, of course, they were).

I cannot feel that Mr Musgrove's attempt to discount the earlier Satan on the score that we are looking at him in Hell (his natural place) and against a background that flatters him ('evil') touches the realities of the case. Surely that is to allow oneself to be swayed by mere words. See p. 144, n.2.

real sense with a 'nature', and without such a basis of reference we are at a loss. We have in what follows a series of levels: we meet Satan now on the one level, now on the other: sometimes he is more like the Satan we knew, sometimes less; but nothing truly explains the shifts and alternations. The 'character', in short, disintegrates into what is really a succession of unrelated moods; and with this disintegration new and inferior techniques begin to enter.

Consider, for an immediate instance, the passage in Book IV, shortly after the 'address to the Sun' soliloquy itself, that describes the irruption of the arch-felon into the garden. Disdaining due entrance he leaps the wall, then flies up on to the Tree of Life and sits there like a cormorant:

> Yet not true Life
> Thereby regaind, but sat devising Death
> To them who liv'd; nor on the vertue thought
> Of that life-giving Plant, but only us'd
> For prospect, what well us'd had bin the pledge
> Of immortalitie. So little knows
> Any, but God alone, to value right
> The good before him, but perverts best things
> To worst abuse, or to thir meanest use.   (IV, 196)

What a fall is here! Here, surely we may say, the poem reaches one of its really low spots, here is *manipulation* with a vengeance. Satan perched on his bough, neglecting his opportunities, put to incidental, momentary use as a sort of illustration to a trivial homily! This is Sunday-school-motto technique. It was mean of Milton to use his Satan so.

There is a recovery almost at once. The Satan who stands 'in gaze' at Adam and Eve (IV, 356) is a Satan restored nearly to his original lineaments, for we accept without strain his momentary rapture at the sight of the pair; and his sadness that such beauty must be destroyed is not too deep. Presently (and the more Satan he) he slips into the mocking vein.

The speech is an interesting one. Mr Empson wonders whether the accepted view of it is wholly right—the view that, from the word 'league' on, it expresses a brutal irony rather in the manner of Satan's address to his artillerymen during the war in heaven. Satan, he suggests, may genuinely mean his offer. The devils can carry on life in hell: perhaps man can too: Satan at any rate is not in a position to know that he cannot. So when he says:

> League with you I seek,
> And mutual amitie so streight, so close,
> That I with you must dwell, or you with me
> Henceforih; my dwelling haply may not please
> Like this fair Paradise, your sense, yet such
> Accept your Makers work; he gave it to me,
> Which I as freely give; Hell shall unfould,
> To entertain you two, her widest Gates,
> And send forth all her Kings, (iv, 376)

he may be half or wholly sincere. Mr Empson draws attention, in particular, to the ring of the last three lines: 'their melancholy and their grandeur is that of Milton's direct statements; he does not use all, his key word, for any but a wholesale and unquestioned emotion; what we are to feel here is the ruined generosity of Satan and the greatness of the fate of man.'[1]

I do not think the interpretation can possibly hold, though the three lines that Mr Empson speaks of have, without any question, the effect he describes. The tone takes on, for the moment, a more direct eloquence than is really appropriate, the irony for the moment seems to disappear. It is not, surely, intentional. It is simply that Milton, slightly forgetful, injects just a little too much power—power, at least, of the wrong sort—so that we note a difference. If the three lines (or as much of them as Mr Empson quotes) ended the passage, his conjecture would be more plausible: but they do not. The passage continues:

> there will be room,
> Not like these narrow limits, to receive
> Your numerous ofspring; if no better place...

where the irony, if it was ever lost, comes back with a rush.

[1] Some Versions of Pastoral (1935), p. 168.

But perhaps it is true (if one looks very closely at it) that the speech does not make a perfect imaginative whole: that between the different elements of it there is a faint but real discord. Satan's feeling, up to the word 'league', has a kind of reality. He is really impressed, really sad, really regretful. And then his visage changes—too suddenly. It is as if he had slipped on another face, a wolfish one. The verse makes him seem to lick his lips as he looks at the pair: he could squeeze them to death ('mutual amitie so streight, so close'); and the sardonic tone continues until it is broken into by the three lines of unadulterated grandeur. If the grandeur had been sustained any longer it would have been troublesome: we should not have been able to harmonize it with the general drift of the speech. But it ceases now; and the tide of the irony is strong enough to carry us over the interval. It would be pleasant to think that Satan spoke the phrase 'public reason just', towards the end of his speech, with a sarcastic glitter in his eye—a 'leer malign'—but it is unsafe to think so. Milton catches up and carries on the phrase in his own quite serious comment:

> So spake the Fiend, and with necessitie,
> The Tyrants plea, excus'd his devilish deeds.

The passage is interesting in one further way. Here, superficially at least, is conflict; here could be drama.

> And should I at your harmless innocence
> Melt, as I doe....

The late Professor Elton felt that the moment really was dramatic. 'He goes back, if only in fancy, upon his purpose.'[1] It is true, of course, that he does: but it *is* only in fancy. The reality of the speech we feel, surely, to be in the mockery, and this is partly because we relate it, with such certainty and immediacy, to the Satan of the earlier books.

Indeed I find it impossible, now or at any other point in

[1] *The English Muse* (1933), p. 239.

the poem, to feel that the 'real tragedy' (as Professor Elton expressed it) is being 'played out in the breast of Satan'.[1] The simple truth, as it seems to me, is that we cannot believe sufficiently (for reasons already discussed) in the reality of the conflicts adumbrated. This speech, and the great soliloquy at the opening of the book, give us glimpses of a tragedy that might have been—if the foundations for it had ever really been laid. The elements of tragic characterization are here; they are forever approaching, forever drawing together, but no spark can fuse them. The 'tragedy' of Satan is essentially a shadow-show: he is put through the motions of a tragic conflict, that is all. In the whole of his history, I would suggest, there is no moment of drama comparable to the moment when Adam hears Eve's confession and faces his decision: *that* is authentic drama indeed.

From this point on, at any rate, the possibility of genuine tragedy becomes less and less; and, conversely, Milton's *interference* in the presentation becomes more and more marked. Satan is very much himself again in the interview with Zephon and Ithuriel. 'Not to know mee argues your selves unknown': this is his old form regained. But Milton will not let him be —cannot, indeed, afford to—for there is only one way now of keeping the contract of the poem, and that is by energetically pressing Satan down and down. So he is made to be 'abasht' by the youthful Cherub (IV, 846). It was not like the Satan we knew to let himself be abashed by anyone, and Milton himself seems to have but little faith in what he has written, for he follows immediately with a second, and much more plausible, cause for Satan's discomfiture:

> but chiefly to find here observd
> His lustre visibly impar'd.   (IV, 849)

The progressive impairment of the lustre, however, is merely another kind of 'interference', taking us a step farther on the

1 Op. cit. p. 239.

road to downright allegory: as is Satan's 'imbruting' of himself in animal forms. He feels his disgrace in this, it is said. He is made to, of course.

> O foul descent! that I who erst contended
> With Gods to sit the highest, am now constraind
> Into a Beast, and mixt with bestial slime,
> This essence to incarnate and imbrute,
> That to the hight of Deitie aspir'd;
> But what will not Ambition and Revenge
> Descend to? who aspires must down as low
> As high he soard, obnoxious first or last
> To basest things. (IX, 163)

But the passage illustrates pointedly enough how far we have travelled from the character and quality of the first books. Satan has become hardly more than a helpless symbol, an exhibit, endowed with the capacity to point his own moral. This second 'passion' soliloquy is surely in a different realm of art from the opening addresses of Satan, and the short 'stupidly good' soliloquy, a little later, is no improvement on it. Both are somewhat clumsily information-giving ('Of these the vigilance I dread', 'for I view far round'), and in the second, as in the first, Satan is in the position very much of a patient who is being forced hypnotically to insult himself. The allegorical vein has developed still farther, and we learn that pain has made inroads in Satan's strength. The true 'degeneration' is not in Satan but in the method.

The final stage is in some respects the most interesting of all, and it tells the whole story of what has been happening. This is the scene of the transformation of the bad angels into serpents and the chewing of the ashes, the true technical nature of which has never, as far as I know, been pointed out. The technique of this famous scene is the technique of the comic cartoon. This is not just a way of being rude to Milton. It is most interesting to observe that the technique of it is *exactly* that of the comic cartoon. The method of the cartoon is to allow the villain of the piece to reach a pitch of high confidence and vainglory, and then to dash him down. The whole point is that he is dashed down, the essence of cartoon-technique being to bring your adversary to grief by unfair means—in short, by some form of practical joke. This, of course, is precisely how Satan is treated here. What happens to him parallels in the exactest manner what used to happen in religious plays to the Devil and Herod, what happens in war-posters to our enemies, and what happens in film comedies to the Big Bad Wolf. Milton of course does it superbly, and it is hardly necessary to add that in sheer verbal power and expressiveness the passage has scarcely its match in *Paradise Lost*. And the construction of it, the timing, are as masterly: each ludicrous, uproarious calamity being succeeded by another still more ludicrous and uproarious, until the climax is reached with the final 'aggravation' (in both senses of the word the very essence of the art of cartoon) and the miserable tricked victims begin to eat.

It is a scene we would not give up for worlds, but to treat such a scene (as would seem to be usually done) as if it were in sober verity the conclusion and climax of a valid development is surely to lapse into a critical absurdity. To attempt to link such a scene as this with what happens in the first two books of *Paradise Lost* is to try to bring incommensurables together, for the kind of art exemplified in this passage and the kind of art with which the presentment of Satan began have simply no meeting-point. They are in different realms of discourse. The scene is amusing, and the writing of it is superb: but about Satan it proves literally nothing whatever.

I finish the chapter with a note on Milton's Hell, which has some peculiar features.

Theology supplies us with a diversity of hells, but they all, I think, have one quality in common. Whether the punishments are conceived literally or not, whether the true suffering is in the mind or the body, whether the pain itself is continuous or intermittent, whatever the internal economy of hell may be: in a true hell the damned have come to the end of their road; hell is their terminus. What activity remains for them is of the nature of a meaningless round, an endless marking-time:

> saxum ingens volvunt alii, radiisve rotarum
> districti pendent: sedet aeternumque sedebit
> infelix Theseus.

That is the true type of hell. In the *Inferno* it is the same. The sinners symbolize their sin through all eternity, perpetually relive the past, or else stay fixed—grotesque mounted specimens—in horrible parody of their guilt. Without such fixity, literal or in effect, hell loses most of its meaning.

This is precisely what Milton's Hell does. While Milton desired to make his Hell impressive as a place of punishment (drawing local colour for it, legitimately enough, from his classical precedents) he also desired, somewhat inconsistently, to cram it as full as he possibly could with human interest. This was for the good of the poem, and the result is superb. But what in the meantime happens to Hell as such? It is obvious that as the conclave proceeds Hell, for all the effective pressure it exerts on our consciousness, has as good as vanished. The livid flames become mere torches to light the assembly of the powers. A little later, when there is leisure, Milton recollects his duty, resumes his account of the infernal landscape and adds further items to his (somewhat meagre) list of tortures. But as he has just proved to us in the clearest way how little the rebels are inconvenienced by their situation it is impossible for us to take these further lurid descriptions very seriously. The plain fact of it, of course, is that Milton's Hell is very much a nominal one: it is less a hell than a vast concentration camp: less even that than a vast, remote, somewhat gloomy and uncomfortable shelter where the defeated rebels can rest, recover their strength and 'regroup'.

It is really very curious to note how little the bad angels *are* inconvenienced.

> Part curb thir fierie Steeds, or shun the Goal
> With rapid wheels, or fronted Brigads form.   (II, 531)

We might be in the Elysian fields, where we most decidedly should not be. It is as if for the moment Milton were thinking (improperly) in terms of Hades. The details, in fact, if we care to dwell on them, become very confusing. What are the conditions in Hell supposed to be? There is of course a kind of lull during Books I and II—there has to be one. Conditions, we understand from various remarks, were much worse before we arrived on the scene and may become much worse later on; that is partly why Belial advises extreme caution: better not stir God up. Yet conditions, even while the action is in progress, are (theoretically) bad enough: 'torture without end Still urges' (I, 67); 'these raging fires Will slack'n, if his breath stir not thir flames' (II, 213); in spite of which, organized field sports are possible. The reason for these and other vaguenesses in the picture is fairly evident: Milton was trying his best to accomplish two incompatible things at the same time. He wanted to convey, as far as he could, the effect of a genuine hell; but he also wanted, still more, to make the drama in Hell intense. Hell therefore as a locality has to serve a double duty: it is a place of perpetual and unceasing punishment, in theory; and it is also, in the practice of the poem, an assembly ground, a military area, a base for future operations. The two conceptions do not very well agree.

But the chief un-hell-like characteristic of Milton's Hell is simply the atmosphere of busy planning, of life nearly as lively as ever, of energies unquenched. The legitimate Hell in *Paradise Lost* is the Hell that is conveyed in such lines as

> A Dungeon horrible, on all sides round
> As one great Furnace flam'd, yet from those flames
> No light, but rather darkness visible

> Serv'd only to discover sights of woe,
> Regions of sorrow, doleful shades, where peace
> And rest can never dwell, hope never comes
> That comes to all;   (i, 61)

or

>   and feel by turns the bitter change
> Of fierce extreams, extreams by change more fierce,
> From Beds of raging Fire to starve in Ice
> Thir soft Ethereal warmth, and there to pine
> Immovable, infixt, and frozen round,
> Periods of time, thence hurried back to fire.   (ii, 598)

But amid the teeming interests of Books i and ii such passages make on us only a minor and insignificant impression. They are merely the setting, of which for most of the time we are naturally oblivious, for the great consult: not much more than a decorative fringe or border, attended to by Milton when his more pressing preoccupations allow. And the plain truth about the giant personalities who absorb all our interest here—who take up their lives pretty well at the point where they left them, who persist in their natures, who preserve their energies and wills, who plan for the future, who mean at the very least to make themselves comfortable, who feel no remorse—is that they have never in any true sense been in 'hell' at all.

For this reason, and for others, I do not see how Mr Lewis's ingenious modern analogies for the states of the fallen angels can possibly hold. 'Each of them is like a man who has just sold his country or his friend and now knows himself to be a pariah.'[1] But do the rebels, in fact, feel that they have 'sold' anything? Not one of them feels guilt. They are in a painful position, defeated, that is all: the only true modern analogy, surely, is with *that*. There is not the slightest moral resemblance between Moloch and a traitor who sees the true nature of his deed and whose impulse is to 'rush blind-headed' at the thing he has wronged; or between Belial and a false lover who in 'one last unforgettable conversation' with the

1 Op. cit. p. 101.

woman he has cheated sees himself as he is and perceives all he is losing. Moloch is angry because he has been ejected from a good place where he thinks he still has a right to be —that is all. Belial is not sorry, except for the fact that the war has landed him and his fellows in this plight; he does not shrink from the thought of what he did, he is not bothered in the slightest about the true quality of his offence: he is miserable, that is all. Mr Lewis's chapter on 'Satan's Followers' is, I would suggest, of the nature, not so much of criticism, as of a sermon—an extremely suggestive and stimulating sermon, to be sure. A sermon is entitled to use its text less as a subject for rigorous interpretation than as a convenient springboard for disquisition on moral truths. Mr Lewis, I think, uses the followers of Satan in very much the same way. And though he anticipates and meets the charge that he is treating the poem for the moment as allegory, that, I think, is what he is really doing all the same: only in that way could the analogues he bring forward become valid.

CHAPTER V

GOD AND THE ANGELS—AND DANTE

In Milton's God we have over again, but in a much heightened form, the problem of his Adam. The difficulty is obvious: perfection, quite strictly, is unportrayable, for as soon as the process of portrayal begins we, the readers, begin a corresponding, and quite involuntary and irresistible, process of translation; we translate into the terms of limitation and imperfection. Indeed, the translation in a sense is already effected for us, for the portrayal itself is translation. There is no way of avoiding this process, but in certain circumstances and by skilful management it can be checked and minimized. Strong pressure can sometimes be brought to bear on us to discount the human responses that rise in our minds inevitably, when someone in our own likeness is placed before us in a work of literature. For example, no one can read the *Paradiso* without noting and filing away (the process need not be very conscious) natural, spontaneous, human impressions of Beatrice. If the actual womanly nature of Beatrice were at all in question these impressions would be very important; some of them might be disturbing. She could seem to us unlikeable in certain respects—sharp, sententious and 'difficult'. She *is* 'difficult'—if we allow the natural picture of her to form. But, as a rule, we do not allow it to form. We counteract, even as they take shape, impressions that we feel instinctively would jar with the effect that Dante is intending. This docility is induced in us by the tact of Dante. It is true that he has not succeeded in inducing such docility everywhere and at all times and with all his readers. He did not succeed very well, for example, with John Addington Symonds. Symonds could not by any shifts bring himself to terms with Beatrice: taking her naturally he found himself faced with a woman preacher, taking her allegorically he found himself faced with a stiff automaton. But most of us manage: and we do so because Dante is so successful in managing *us*.

Milton is not so good a manager, and his problem, in any case, was harder. This time we are not nearly so ready to acquiesce in the clear intentions of the poet—to concede him what he wishes or to meet him halfway; and our refractoriness is not solely or even chiefly due to any dislike we may happen to entertain for Milton's theological position. Mr Lewis is surely right when he says that 'the theological flaws (however we assess them) would not be *poetically* disastrous if only Milton had shown more poetical prudence'.[1] Everything, certainly, hinged on the prudence or imprudence of the treatment, and Mr Lewis, I think, goes to the heart of the matter (though not perhaps quite in the way he intended) when he proceeds: 'A God, theologically speaking, much worse than Milton's, would escape criticism if only He had been made sufficiently awful, mysterious and vague. When the poet is content to suggest, our theological scruples are cast to the winds. When we read

> About him all the Sanctities of Heaven
> Stood thick as Starrs, and from his sight receiv'd
> Beatitude past utterance   (III, 60)

or

> Dark with excessive bright thy skirts appeer   (III, 380)

we are silenced.'[2] This is true: these are examples of the really prudent treatment of God. But it will be observed that what Mr Lewis is really saying as he defends the God of Milton is that the closer this God approaches the vanishing-point the better he becomes; and this, again, is perfectly true. That, indeed, was the tactful, prudent method of Dante with God—to keep him hidden: to lead us towards him, it may be,

1 Op. cit. p. 126.   2 Ibid.

by degrees of mounting suspense, but to refuse the final
revelation. Mr Lewis appears to me to be not quite accurate
in his comparisons here. Speaking of the anthropomorphic
details in Milton 'that make the Divine laughter sound
merely spiteful and the Divine rebukes querulous', he adds:
'that they need not have sounded like this, Dante and the
Hebrew prophets show.'[1] But there is no Divine laughter
(however inoffensive) and there are no Divine rebukes
(however benevolent) in Dante: rebukes and laughter from
God are precisely what Dante will not risk. Nor is it quite
true, surely, to say that while Dante in the last canto is
'himself looking at God and inviting us to look with him',
Milton 'has only to describe how the angels and Adam
looked at God',[2] so that we see all of them, as it were, in
profile. The contrast, as Mr Lewis expresses it, seems to me
to misstate, to the point of reversing, the methods of the
two poets. The *Divine Comedy*, doubtless, is a religious poem
in a sense in which *Paradise Lost* is not. But can we truly
be said to 'look at God' in Dante? If we had been made to
look at him the effect of the last canto, instead of being
what we know it is, would most certainly have been calamitous
in the extreme. We look at the screens and dazzling symbols
of him, and we look at these through the eyes of one whose
faculties, strengthened though they were, hardly bore the
sight; and the sight itself we do not behold directly, but as
imperfectly recovered and reshaped by the fainting human
memory. This was the thrice-guarded method of Dante.
Milton's method is exactly opposite, for while it is true that
Paradise Lost is an *action* in a sense in which the *Divine Comedy*
is not—an action in which we see God playing a part along
with man and angels—it by no means follows that we ourselves
do not look at him, or look at him only (so to say) in profile.
It would be difficult to imagine a more thoroughly frontal
look at God than one of his self-justifying soliloquies in

1 Op. cit. p. 127.   2 Ibid. p. 128

Paradise Lost affords: such soliloquies as these are nothing less than invitations to us to stare God full in the face. It is Milton, not Dante, who takes all the risks; it is he, not Dante, who dares the cruel, direct, unshaded vision.

It is not difficult, at any rate, to understand why that suppression of ordinary human responses, so possible in the *Divine Comedy* as we read of Beatrice, is not possible in *Paradise Lost* as we read of God. In the first place, the indications are so frequent, full and emphatic, the human traits in the portrait are so deeply etched, that there is no escaping them even if we would. With the best will in the world, we cannot avoid Milton's God or refuse to react to him: he is too obstinately there. And this is partly because Milton wanted him to be there; for it is not as if he made much attempt at any point to use the tactics that Mr Lewis notes as desirable—suggesting his God, screening him, risking him reluctantly (as one risks a capital ship). On the contrary Milton uses him as if no dangers were to be imagined, and is quite unhesitant in the traits he imparts to him. Nor is it to be forgotten that some of the traits to which we object appealed to Milton: they are not there by accident or (so to say) as the by-products of an impossible delineation; they are there because Milton deliberately put them there, because he *liked* God in just that way.

The situation, then, was complex; and yet it is a recurrent wonder that Milton should have been quite content with what he had done, that his ear, even if insensitive to the subtler discords, should not have caught some of the harsher and more jarring notes. The start is bad:

> So stretcht out huge in length the Arch-fiend lay
> Chain'd on the burning Lake, nor ever thence
> Had ris'n or heav'd his head, but that the will
> And high permission of all-ruling Heaven
> Left him at large to his own dark designs
> That with reiterated crimes he might
> Heap on himself damnation.   (I, 209)

This is unamiable, to say the least of it; and the effect is not lessened by Milton's extraordinary carelessness (a carelessness that at times is not less than insulting to his readers) in matching his facts and seeing to it that his poem, from moment to moment, at least makes sense. God addresses the Son:

> Onely begotten Son, seest thou what rage
> Transports our adversarie, whom no bounds
> Prescrib'd, no barrs of Hell, nor all the chains
> Heapt on him there, nor yet the main Abyss
> Wide interrupt can hold; so bent he seems
> On desperat revenge, that shall redound
> Upon his own rebellious head. And now
> Through all restraint broke loose he wings his way
> Not farr off Heav'n, in the Precincts of light.... (III, 80)

Has Milton forgotten, or has he counted on our forgetting, that it was through the 'sufferance of supernal Power' (I, 241) (not, as they flattered themselves, through 'their own recover'd strength') that Satan and his mate have 'scap't the Stygian flood' at all, and that Satan was deliberately unchained in order that he might triple-dye himself in crime? The intrinsic difficulties of the task were grave enough, in all conscience. It is hard not to feel some slight impatience with a poet who prefers to double them: who, not content with a God who *must*, however matters are contrived, appear somewhat vindictive, goes out of his way to convict him on his very first appearance of flagrant disingenuousness and hypocrisy.

The address that follows this preamble shows Milton worried, or at least uneasy. This is God's long speech of self-justification, the speech in which he defends himself for actions past and forestalls possible criticism of actions yet to come:

> So will fall
> Hee and his faithless Progenie: whose fault?
> Whose but his own? ingrate, he had of mee
> All he could have; I made him just and right,
> Sufficient to have stood, though free to fall.
> Such I created all th' Ethereal Powers
> And Spirits, both them who stood & them who faild;

Freely they stood who stood, and fell who fell.
Not free, what proof could they have givn sincere
Of true allegiance, constant Faith or Love,
Where onely what they needs must do, appeard,
Not what they would? what praise could they receive?
What pleasure I from such obedience paid,
When Will and Reason (Reason also is choice)
Useless and vain, of freedom both despoild,
Made passive both, had servd necessitie,
Not mee. They therefore as to right belongd,
So were created, nor can justly accuse
Thir maker, or thir making, or thir Fate;
As if Predestination over-rul'd
Thir will, dispos'd by absolute Decree
Or high foreknowledge; they themselves decreed
Thir own revolt, not I: if I foreknew,
Foreknowledge had no influence on their fault,
Which had no less prov'd certain unforeknown.
So without least impulse or shadow of Fate,
Or aught by me immutablie foreseen,
They trespass, Authors to themselves in all
Both what they judge and what they choose; for so
I formed them free, and free they must remain,
Till they enthrall themselves: I else must change
Thir nature, and revoke the high Decree
Unchangeable, Eternal, which ordain'd
Thir freedom, they themselves ordain'd thir fall.
The first sort by thir own suggestion fell,
Self-tempted, self-deprav'd: Man falls deceiv'd
By the other first: Man therefore shall find grace,
The other none: in Mercy and Justice both,
Through Heav'n and Earth, so shall my glorie excel,
But Mercy first and last shall brightest shine.   (III, 95)

It is not much use attacking the logic of this, though the logic is vulnerable enough. The human impression is what is important; and in that respect the speech could be regarded, I suppose, as nearly the standard example of what is likely to occur when the supreme risk is taken of permitting a theoretically perfect character to dilate on his own impeccability. The speech yields a perfect picture of an immaculate character on the defensive. If Milton had been trying to do this very thing he could not have succeeded in conveying a clearer impression of nervousness, insecurity and doubt. The uneasy explanations, the hammering in of key words ('they themselves', 'they themselves', 'not I'), the anxiety to meet beforehand all possible lines of attack, the rhetorical pleading, the indignation before the event ('whose fault? Whose but his own? ingrate', etc): we could not counter such impressions even if we would; they are too strong for us to deny. 'Mercy' comes in at the finish by an almost comical afterthought—in the very nick of time. And it is in response to such words as these that the blessed spirits (like Dante's elect) feel new joy suffusing them and that ambrosial fragrance fills all heaven.

The truth of course is obvious—there is little need to insist on it again—that it does not come very naturally to Milton to suggest a loving God. Let him try and the tone will presently seem to change despite him, and soon we are back in the groove of divine egoism.

> Man shall not quite be lost, but sav'd who will,
> Yet not of will in him, but grace in me
> Freely voutsaft; once more I will renew
> His lapsed powers, though forfeit and enthrall'd
> By sin to foul exorbitant desires;
> Upheld by me, yet once more he shall stand
> On even ground against his mortal foe,
> By me upheld, that he may know how frail
> His fall'n condition is, and to me ow
> All his deliv'rance, and to none but me.   (III, 173)

It is true that in the speech of the Son, just before, there had been a real lightening towards mercy, and that the Father had seemed for the moment to respond. Nevertheless the burden of the reply is still Justice. Milton writes with more conviction (quite accurately, with more real sympathy) when he comes to the concluding lines of it, which carry the real point of the whole:

> Die hee or Justice must; unless for him
> Som other able, and as willing, pay
> The rigid satisfaction, death for death.   (III, 210)

In such lines Milton seems more comfortable: 'rigid satisfaction' is the kind of phrase he likes to turn, has all the
weight of his personal emphasis behind it.

And then comes the fiasco (for why, after all, should we
not make the point?) of God's call for a volunteer, and that
heavy silence in heaven while the angels, stricken mute, weigh
pros and cons:

> on mans behalf
> Patron or Intercessor none appeerd,
> Much less that durst upon his own head draw
> The deadly forfeiture, and ransom set.   (III, 219)

Dramatically the moment is very good, and the Son has his
great opportunity. But what a risk! Who but Milton would
have ventured to expose the Heavenly Quire itself to such a
choice!

There is no need, at this time of day, to follow the progress
of the delineation. It could be put almost into a formula.
The utterance of God is good in proportion as it is drained
of personality: the less we *feel* God in what he says the better
is the effect. The majestic passage describing the 'dread
Tribunal' of the Son (III, 326) is an instance. We listen to
a full-toned Voice from the void. But personality, unluckily,
is forever returning. God in Book v is still looking for ways
to render man inexcusable, still anxious lest he should be able
to pretend 'surprisal unforewarned'. Indeed, never to the
end of the poem does God succeed in living down this
particular worry. The speech of derision (v, 717) and the
Son's speech of flattery in reply merely underline, again, the
sheer impossibility of the task: at this stage we expect Milton
to founder at any moment, begin to feel that it is by a miracle
that his God has not yet sunk the poem.

One passage in Book VIII for a special reason deserves a
comment: it exemplifies pointedly the curious ill-luck that
seems to dog the portraiture: nothing, apparently, *can* go
right with it. Raphael at this point has the duty of listening

to Adam's story of the beginning of human life (so that we ourselves may hear it) and must first plausibly explain why he does not know the facts already. The simplest explanation is that he was not there when the creation of man took place, and that accordingly is what he is made to say:

> For I that Day was absent, as befell,
> Bound on a voyage uncouth and obscure,
> Farr on excursion toward the Gates of Hell;
> Squar'd in full Legion (such command we had)
> To see that none thence issu'd forth a spie,
> Or enemie, while God was in his work,
> Least hee incenst at such eruption bold,
> Destruction with Creation might have mixt.   (VIII, 229)

So far so good, except perhaps for the startling impression of the unpredictable consequences of God's temper. But at this point of his writing Milton remembers that no spy *can* issue forth from Hell unless with God's knowledge and by his permission. So he adds:

> Not that they durst without his leave attempt,
> But us he sends upon his high behests
> For state, as Sovran King, and to enure
> Our prompt obedience.

This is sheer improvisation: ten lines back Milton knew no more than anybody else that in a moment or two he would be picturing God as a military martinet whose hobby is drill, and who likes to inflict useless missions on his men 'for state', and to see that they jump smartly into action at the word of command. He has merely drifted into such a picture because one thing led to another. Raphael's explanation was not properly thought out, and had to be capped by a second. But this second explanation is not very good either: in fact in its implications it is very bad. But Milton is deep in the tangle now and makes no further efforts. Why, after all, we wonder, should we pain ourselves to defend the God of Milton when Milton himself refuses to take even elementary care?

Looking back, it is interesting to speculate on what might have been. Could Milton have produced a warmer, more 'human', God? Sir Herbert Grierson thinks he might have done so if he had been capable of reading the Hebrew prophets with a fuller sympathy; they could have taught him that it was possible to conceive a God 'who denounces sin' and who yet really appears to 'yearn over His children'.[1] But the story was given, and the facts of this story, when all is said, were against God. The tendency of the myth was awkward. It would have been difficult in this context, with whatever finesse, to have made God completely acceptable. 'Thy terms too hard', 'inexplicable Thy justice seems': most readers, perhaps, are inclined to echo Adam's arraignment and to feel that he gives up in the end rather easily:

> Him after all Disputes
> Forc't I absolve.   (x, 828)

At any rate *we* are under no obligation to absolve Milton, merely because the problem was difficult. He is often rash, often careless, and the element of sheer clumsiness in the portrait is not to be ignored.

Johnson was not quite accurate in his account of Milton's angels. He found, as we know, a 'confusion of spirit and matter' pervading Milton's whole narrative of the war in Heaven. Johnson wrote as if Milton had been occupied purely and simply in finding the best solution to a technical problem. It was obvious that 'immateriality could supply him no images', so he invested his angels with form and matter. But having done so, Johnson maintained, he should have kept immateriality out of sight, made his choice properly. Instead, we alternate between 'pure spirit' and 'animated body'—do not quite know where we stand. And the reason, according to Johnson, is that Milton allowed his 'philosophy'

1 Op. cit. p. 110.

(that is to say, his real belief about the angels) to intrude into his poetry and to perplex it.

The point that Johnson missed (as Mr Lewis has emphasized again) is that Milton *did* believe in the kind of angels he drew. Early in the poem (1, 425) we are given a description of their 'soft and uncompounded' essence, and before the war begins we are told at considerable length about the 'various forms, various degrees' of substance (v, 473), about the scale of nature, about the means by which body may 'up to spirit work', and have had the notion that Raphael did not eat, or ate only seemingly, put in its right place for us as just the 'common gloss Of Theologians'. Milton, that is to say, when he pictured the angels as corporeal in a sort is not merely taking the nearest way out of a technical difficulty; he is also letting us know what, in his considered opinion, are the strong probabilities of the case. I suppose we need a slightly less positive word than 'belief'. There is one passage, indeed, that would appear for the moment to imply that Milton is doing precisely what Johnson took him to be doing: finding the readiest solution to a technical problem, using poetic fictions in order to express the inexpressible. Raphael wonders:

> how shall I relate
> To human sense th' invisible exploits
> Of warring Spirits   (v, 564)

and warns Adam of the technique he intends to adopt:

> what surmounts the reach
> Of human sense, I shall delineate so,
> By lik'ning spiritual to corporal forms,
> As may express them best, though what if Earth
> Be but the shaddow of Heav'n, and things therein
> Each to other like, more then on earth is thought?   (v, 571)

There would appear to be at least some degree of hesitation in the passage: Milton obviously is not prepared to go to the stake for his belief in the materiality of angels. The angelic lore, conveyed so flatly and confidently in Book 1 here appears as something rather less forthright and certain. Nevertheless, the general impression[1] of the various passages is very clear, and the concluding lines of Raphael's speech reinforce it. Milton when he describes angels in action is not, as Johnson seemed to think, accommodating 'pure spirit' to the necessities of a narrative poem, or is not doing that only; he is at the same time giving what seems to him a credible version of the angelic nature.

What follows? Mr Lewis's view would seem to be that, this point settled, the rest is all plain sailing, that the difficulties to which Johnson was leading are automatically eliminated. I do not think they are. The plain fact is that Milton's view of angels (Mr Lewis lists the forerunners and contemporaries with whom he shared it) was rather nonsensical, and that in such a detailed treatment as he designed it was almost impossible to keep the nonsense in it out of sight. It is not, of course, as if he makes any attempt to keep it out of sight. As always, he fears nothing. There is not a latent embarrassment in the theory that he is not at pains to drag to light. The puzzles of digestion, elimination, 'sex'—he is determined to draw our attention to them all. There is not an awkward question that he is not resolute to raise. And for all this it is only fair that he should pay due penalty in our mockery. The fact that he believed in his absurdities—or was willing to risk suggesting that he did— surely has the effect of rendering them rather *more* (not, as Mr Lewis thinks, less) reprehensible; for in that case it was incumbent on him, not only as a literary craftsman doing his best in difficult circumstances, but also as a reasonable human being, to demonstrate that his ideas, when worked

[1] Not affected seriously, I think, by what Mr P. L. Carver has said of the possible influence of Tertullian and of St Thomas Aquinas ('The Angels in *Paradise Lost*', *The Review of English Studies*, October, 1940, p. 415). Mr Carver has an interesting note on the word 'mist': 'nor seemingly The Angel, nor in mist.'

out in detail, could make at least some show of coherence and common sense.[1]

The war in Heaven is on rather a different footing from the accounts of angelic digestive processes (for which there was only the thinnest of pretexts) or the excursus into the mysteries of angelic copulation (for which there was no real excuse at all). The war had to be described, and it involved questions that could not altogether be allowed to lie. Johnson failed, perhaps, to define quite accurately the source of the confusion in this narrative, but his drift was right. The radical incongruity surely lies in this, that Milton, having laid down certain theoretic bases for what he is about to do, proceeds then in almost every detail of his description to stultify them. It is important to remember that the theory of angels that Milton held is only loosely to be described as the 'corporeal': if he had held a theory that could have been truly described by that word there would have been no confusion in the narrative of the war. He believed, of course, or professed to believe, that the angelic substance was a strange mixture or compromise, not spirit, not matter, but a soft intermediate indeterminate 'essence', with properties that he ventures to formulate. To say that the Miltonic angels are corporeal is rather like saying that a jellyfish has a body in the sense in which a human being has one. If we pin him down to his words Johnson was wrong in saying that Milton confused spirit and matter; but he would have been right if he had said that Milton confused 'x-matter' with matter (the 'x-matter' being the queer substance of angels, so different from 'gross' matter as we know it); and this 'x-matter'

---

1 Mr Lewis seems to me to accord an undue respect to the lucubrations of Milton's authorities in these matters—and to Milton's own theories. They give us the glimpses, he says, 'which contemporary *scientific* imagination thought it had attained of a life going on just above the human level' (op. cit. p. 111). Seventeenth-century science can do better than this. At any rate, if Milton was trying to be scientific he must take the consequences.

is so near, on occasion, to spirit that there is really little to choose between the two. The fact that Satan was able to enter and animate the toad proved to Johnson that Satan was able to assume for the moment the qualities of spirit. Mr Lewis says that this is not so: the animation of the toad does not prove that Satan is immaterial, but only that his subtle body can penetrate a grosser body and contract itself to very small dimensions. It seems a distinction without a very great difference. The truth surely is that Johnson uses the word 'spirit' partly because of a deficiency of language. (A part of his worry also, it will be remembered, was about the spear and shield.) The logic of the whole matter would seem to be this: Milton having posited, not corporeality, but this special kind of angelic corporeality for which we have no name, and having to some extent laid down the laws of it, should then, to be consistent, have gone on to plan his warfare in terms of it. Actually, of course, he does nothing of the sort. He feels (naturally) that Homeric battles are prescribed, yet nothing is more obvious than that for such beings as these, with their powers of dilatation, contraction and so on, Homeric battles are (so to say) an anachronism. Mr Lewis says that there was nothing unreasonable in giving the angels armour. I think there was. Milton *had* to give them armour, of course, once having conceived the battles in Homeric terms: but I do not think the armour can be defended on grounds of reason: such a line of defence is surely hopeless. It would have been much better for the angels to dodge, as their mishaps sufficiently show. By resorting to clumsy devices appropriate for the protection of 'gross' bodies (which theirs are not) they sacrifice at a stroke every physical and tactical advantage that their special 'essence' conferred.

The result, if Milton *had* used his theories consistently, could only have been, I suppose, some weird Wellsian scene. Yet even something of that kind could hardly have been more grotesque than certain of the passages of arms that we behold.

For what happens is that Milton insists equally on both conceptions: he will not allow us to forget for a moment, either that the warfare *is* Homeric, grossly material in its equipment and results, or that the fighters who are waging it have 'bodies' that are not material in the same sense at all, bodies that are quite incongruous with the arms and armour and all the conditions of the war. The result, of course, is to keep the difficulties ever present to us in their acutest form. In the very midst of things we have the elaborate account (VI, 344) prompted by the wounding of Satan of the pervasive vitality of angels, their liquidity of texture, and their power to assume any colour, shape or size, condense or rare, 'as likes them best'. Yet in the next breath Moloch threatens to bind Gabriel and drag him at his chariot wheels. This, when all is said, is treating us very nearly as morons.

It would be interesting to know what Milton's mood precisely was as he wrote this part of his poem. He seems interested at times, yet it would not be strange if he had felt some oppression at the way the work was going just here. The narrative makes a brave show, but only towards the end, with the entry of the Son, does real life come into it: it acquires new zest then, the verse itself seems invigorated, and we are swept to a superb close. But for much of the time Milton seems unhappy, straining for his effects. There is expense of effort for no proportionate result.

> So under fierie Cope together rush'd
> Both Battels maine, with ruinous assault
> And inextinguishable rage.   (VI, 215)

Does this cause a flutter? One's ears become insensitive to the operative words: rage, ruin, dreadful, amazement, destruction, horrid, hideous, confusion. The imagery is grandiose, conventional, unrealized:

> as if on Earth
> Winds under ground or waters forcing way
> Sidelong, had push't a Mountain from his seat
> Half sunk with all his Pines.   (VI, 195)

There are elementary lapses, as if Milton's mind strayed:[1]

> at each behind
> A Seraph *stood*, and in his hand a Reed
> *Stood* waving tipt with fire; while we suspense,
> Collected *stood* within our thoughts amus'd.   (VI, 578)

And the climax is one at which one would like to think that even Milton giggled:

> So Hills amid the Air encountered Hills,
> Hurl'd to and fro with jaculation dire,
> That under ground they fought in dismal shade.   (VI, 664)

The methods of Dante in facing these, or very similar, problems afford instructive comparisons. The analogy, it is true, is by no means perfect, and the comparisons are bound, in some respects, to be unfair to Milton. Milton was compelled to grapple with certain difficulties (the direct presentation of God, for example) that for Dante simply did not arise. Again, Dante's scheme had certain inherent advantages, not the least of which was the obliqueness that is the very key and principle of the visions. Just as the divine rays are slanted from Beatrice to Dante, coming to him as by a second view, so Dante himself, the figure in the poem, refracts to us the sight whether of damnation or purgation or beatitude. This principle of the 'delegated sensibility' (as Henry James might have called it) at one stroke eased the problems—relieving the poet, so to say, of a measure of responsibility—and gave openings that Milton did not by the nature of the case enjoy. Every reader of the *Divine Comedy* knows, for example, the extraordinarily simple, happy, effective technique that Dante uses for *placing* us amongst the shades. It is, of course, to make hardly any attempt to report the effect of the souls, as souls, on him: it is to report his effect on them. Reflect on it, and we see at once that no other method could

1 Unless, of course, the text misrepresents him.

have compared with this in economy of means or in the sharpness of the results obtained; it is an obvious method, yet only a master of narrative would have thought of it. It circumvents at one stroke all the laborious descriptions that Milton, by the nature of his task, was obliged to attempt; it neatly by-passes the central difficulty. A line, a mere phrase, slipped in at this point or that, now accomplishes all that is needed. Dante steps into the skiff of Phlegyas, and the craft, which till then had seemed unfreighted, is pressed deeper into the water; his foot, unlike any other foot in these regions, dislodges stones as he descends the shaky path; his body intercepts the light and the shades stare wonderingly; they watch his throat move in breathing and exclaim as at a strangeness. It is he (and naturally) who in this realm is the marvel, the curiosity, the 'sensation', not they. Having given us our cue in this so simple, yet so effective and startling way, Dante safely leaves us to do the rest.[1] Only once, I think, in the whole of the poem do we come on a passage that reminds us even distantly of Milton's detailed elucidations. This is the speech of Statius in Canto xxv of the *Purgatorio*. Dante has asked how it is that the spirits can be lean, for presumably food, or the lack of it, has no further point or importance in their lives. Statius, starting from the mysteries of conception, proceeds to an account of the embryo, of the joining of soul and body, of the disjoining of them at death, and of the condition then of the disembodied spirit that impresses its semblance on the surrounding air in some such way as light, when it strikes the moisture-laden atmosphere, makes a rainbow: thus the spirit still has form, with apparent senses and faculties. The passage is discreet and suffices to calm incipient questionings. For few readers, whether of Milton or Dante, have an impulse to *make* trouble: we are only too ready to accept, to be quiet, to grant the

1 See some interesting observations on Dante's technique by Professor Stoll in his *Poets and Playwrights*, pp. 282–3.

poet—in reason, and perhaps a little beyond reason—what he wishes. But he, on his side, must not try us too far. If we possibly can believe, we will: we will even stretch a point to believe. But if our good intentions are flouted, we are likely to turn cranky. Dante, in this respect as in so many others, calculates our susceptibilities to a nicety. He knows (what Milton did not) that where a question might really be awkward it is best by far not to raise it: he knows that if *he* does not raise it, we are not likely to do so. His policy in general, therefore, is not to explain.

The same tact informs the later books, and how much, in the *Paradiso* especially, depends on the continued use of that principle of the deputed consciousness! Dante never lets us forget, as we approach the climax, that what he is now seeing is hardly for words to speak, that the flight is too great for human power, that even with the help of the divine grace he can report but a fraction of the truth, that he is in the case of one who wakes from a wondrous dream, who retains the feeling of the dream, it is true, but can never now hope to recapture the dream itself as it was. The poetic intensities of the last canto, the radiance of the language and the perfection of the imagery, would have come to nought, they would indeed not have come into existence, if informing the canto there had not been this supreme literary tact. It is because of it that Dante gives us a sense of ultimate splendour that Milton only rarely, in occasional touches, can suggest.

Dante's method changes subtly between the *Inferno* and the *Purgatorio*, and between that again and the *Paradiso*; and once more the comparisons with *Paradise Lost* are interesting. The *Inferno* is the 'popular' book; upon which Mr Eliot remarks: 'It is apparently easier to accept damnation as poetic material than purgation or beatitude; less is involved that is strange to the modern mind.'[1] This no doubt is true, but the reason

1 *Dante* (1929), p. 36.

why the general instinct makes for the *Inferno* is, I think, less esoteric than Mr Eliot seems to suggest. The *Inferno* is more popular than the *Purgatorio* and the *Paradiso* because its quality is more dramatic than theirs. It is not merely that the book is adventurous, that it is packed with variety, that we never know what is round the next corner. One could almost say that the *principle* of the *Inferno* is drama. And it is curious to note how this is made possible. It is made possible because (much more than in the *Purgatorio* or the *Paradiso*) the human selves of the inmates persist. In a sense, of course, it is this very persistence that constitutes the punishment: to drink for ever the cup of their guilt, to be eternally (if only in bitter parody or burlesque) what they were, to go on doing always what they did—this, as we are made to see again and again, is the very nature of the doom. But if some of the most famous episodes of the *Inferno* are recalled it will be seen that the drama of them is, so to say, irrelevant: this is true of the episode of Farinata and Cavalcanti: the passionate partizanship of the one, the intense paternal love of the other, have nothing strictly to do with the reasons why these men are in hell. What Dante is doing (and this is especially characteristic of the *Inferno*) is allowing himself a precious margin of feeling over and above the guilty passion, for working in. Whether in a strict theory of hell such feeling ought to be there is perhaps debatable: the important fact is that it is this *excess* humanity that gives Dante in the *Inferno* the openings for some of his most thrilling strokes, and for innumerable minor ones the same in kind.

There were fewer opportunities of the sort in the *Purgatorio* and there were almost no opportunities of the sort in the *Paradiso*: this almost followed from the nature of the themes; and Dante modifies his method accordingly. Mr Eliot says of the characters in the *Paradiso*: 'At first, they seem less distinct than the earlier unblessed people; they seem ingeniously varied but fundamentally monotonous variations of insipid blessedness.'[1] Surely they *are* less distinct than the unblessed people; surely they *are* ingeniously varied, but fundamentally monotonous, variations of blessedness. Mr Eliot's real point was that beatitude is as good a theme for poetry as damnation; that is one thing; it is another to say that beatitude can be treated in poetry in the same way as damnation. The fact, at any rate, would seem to be that in the *Paradiso* it is not so treated, and that the particular sort of distinctness that gives the *Inferno* its special character was not really in question here. There are inequalities in Dante's heaven, we know: he tells us there are, and we accept his assurance readily enough. We have, besides, the various categories of the blessed: they are to some extent grouped and classified for us. But to *feel* the diversity of the several states is a different matter altogether and (I would suggest) an impossible feat. Mr Eliot says it is a question of 'gradual adjustment of our vision'.[2] One can only wonder whether he or any other reader of Dante has ever reached the fineness of adjustment necessary for distinguishing the blessedness of the crusaders from the blessedness of the devout scholars, the blessedness of those who have passed their lives in holy retirement from the blessedness of those who have preached, the blessedness of David from the blessedness of the Maccabee, the blessedness of Damiano from the blessedness of Buonaventura. We are in a realm, surely, where individuality, whether in blessedness or anything else, has been extinguished: the souls do not and cannot will anything other or more than the divine will appoints. And this means, in practice, that their personalities, unlike the personalities of the damned, become suppressed or absorbed: very much, indeed, as Dante's own personality is suppressed or absorbed in this part of the poem, for he too, who before had been so various in his emotions (reacting in compassion, amazement, horror, awe, anger, contempt: greeting with shocked pity and

1 Op. cit. pp. 50–1.   2 Ibid. p. 51.

reverence the shade of Brunetto Latini, watching with relish the agony of Argenti, dealing 'toughly' with Bocca) becomes now, as Mr Eliot himself expresses it, 'de- or super-personalized'.

Drama, therefore, drops out, as we can see that it must. The 'characters' in heaven cannot differ (except as one star differeth from another in glory) and that slight margin of excess or surplus humanity that Dante permits himself in the *Inferno*, and from which he gains such extraordinary results, would have been inappropriate here: for obviously the blessed cannot retain the same passionate interest in their past as the damned. Drama drops out, and its place is taken by other things—the poetry of homily, discussion, spectacle, and of what Mr Eliot calls the 'high dream'. It is interesting to note how the proportions of the various elements rearrange themselves. The catalogues are more leisurely now. Amid the bustle of the *Inferno*—so much to see and hear in the time— we had to do with 'brief mentions' of just a few of the damned who are left over in the several categories. And it is perhaps not without significance that it is the *Paradiso* that contains the longest digression in the poem: the episode of Cacciaguida. The method of the *Paradiso*, compared with the method of the *Inferno*, is discursive; it has to be. Such a theme demands —indeed can only be conducted by—a skilled circuitousness. In the *Inferno* Dante is writing about many different kinds of damnation—and they are really different. In the *Paradiso*, though professedly he is describing different kinds of blessedness, in reality he is describing only one kind—for there is only one kind. In a sense, therefore, he can only treat such a theme—as he does—by going about it and about, by large circlings and detours. It is true that we are brought back continually to the central line, the line of feeling, represented by the recurrent and mounting bursts of ecstasy. As the poem draws near to its finish this line is unbroken. But if we had been on it all the time a *Paradiso* of thirty-three cantos would have been an impossibility.

If we study the diverse methods of the *Divine Comedy* and note the principles underlying them, we shall recognize, I think, that these are the same as the principles that explain, among other things, why Satan is the most impressive person in *Paradise Lost*, why drama is enacted in Milton's Hell but not in his Heaven, and why Adam and Eve become characters only after the Fall.

CHAPTER VI

'UNCONSCIOUS MEANINGS' IN
PARADISE LOST

IT was Dr Tillyard who first, in a systematic survey, brought clearly forward the notion of 'unconscious' meanings in *Paradise Lost*, meanings that we may classify and arrange in very much the same way as we do the 'conscious', his suggestion being that between the two sets we have a fair hope of estimating the real significance of the poem. But in a short essay, written early in the century and republished in *Shelburne Essays* (Fourth Series), Paul Elmer More had advanced a similar idea, and had made a proposal about the total meaning of the poem that Dr Tillyard, in a qualified way, finds himself able to absorb into his own account.

More lays down a few general principles about epic poetry: it must possess a theme deeply rooted in national belief; the development of this theme must express, more or less symbolically, some universal truth of human nature; and so forth. He finds that Milton met the first of these conditions by choosing the story of Genesis, which was 'a living reality' to the people of his day, and in a sense 'the most truly national theme' at his disposal. But this was not enough: such a subject, 'truly national' at the time as it may have been, could never have sufficed by itself to give the work enduring value. Beneath any such theme must lie, if the creation is to last, 'some great human truth, some appeal to universal human aspirations, decked in the garb of symbolism'. 'The poet himself', More adds, 'may not be fully conscious of this deeper meaning, and the manner of its involution is something quite different from the methods of the so-called school of symbolists, but there it must be, hidden or manifest.'[1]

1 Op. cit. p. 240.

More then, sweeping aside the cobwebs of centuries, proceeds to show where the 'true theme' of *Paradise Lost*, hitherto missed, really lies. 'Sin is not the innermost subject of this epic, nor man's disobedience and fall; these are but the tragic shadows cast about the central light. Justification of the ways of God to man is not the true moral of the plot: this and the whole divine drama are merely the poet's means of raising his conception to the highest generalization. The true theme is Paradise itself; not Paradise lost, but the reality of that "happy rural seat" where the errant tempter beheld

> To all delight of human sense exposed
> In narrow room nature's whole wealth, yea more,
> A heaven on earth.'[1]

More makes the point that the scenes which have to convey this central meaning are placed, with propriety, in the middle books of the epic, 'just as a painter places the most important object of his picture in the centre of his composition and throws upon it the highest light'.[2]

I do not see any reason, though Dr Tillyard does, why such a theory should be accorded very serious notice. It is obvious that Milton presents his Paradise with exquisite appreciation, and nearly as obvious that this appreciation is somehow related to deep needs of his nature. The image of Paradise is, it would seem, related to deep needs of everybody's nature; it affords inner relaxation, release, after trial and tension and effort; and if we press the matter a little further and take the heartfelt imagining of Paradise as signifying, even with Milton, an unconscious yearning back towards some forgotten haven of security—infantile or pre-natal—no harm, perhaps, is done. Milton was a man: the unconscious tendencies that we seem now to detect in man were therefore present in him, and could hardly have failed to impress themselves in secret ways on some passages, at least, of his writing. It is still a long step

1 Op. cit. p. 243.　　　　　　2 Ibid. p. 249.

from such a recognition to the singling out of the paradisal scenes, deeply felt though they are, as constituting the prime stuff and substance of his poem. Many have felt, with equal or greater reason, that scenes of precisely opposite quality express the very heart of what Milton had to say. Critics who claim that *Paradise Lost* exists for Satan, that it is in him and the energy he represents that the imperishable significance of *Paradise Lost* is centred, have on the face of it a better case. It is surely not much to the point here that Paradise occupies a central position in the epic. It would have been very difficult in any epic treatment of the story to have made it occupy any other position: it is central because of the nature of the case, because that was the right, indeed the only place, artistically, for it.

For the rest, More falls back upon the 'pastoral ideal, haunting the imagination of men', Milton's poem being just one instance of the 'ancient ineradicable longing of the human heart for a garden of innocence, a paradise of idyllic delights, a region to which come only "golden days" fruitful of golden deeds'.[1] We may allow readily enough that this particular longing is ancient and ineradicable, and yet feel strongly that some hurt is done to the due proportions of things when the whole of literature, including Shakespeare, is seen to be just one long illustration of it. 'Shakespeare's sweetest scenes are devoted to the idyllic Forest of Arden and to Perdita's shepherd home.'[2] The truth is that More has a pet fancy about *Paradise Lost*: his thesis deserves no weightier word: and he proceeds to maintain it by selecting ingeniously every trifle that seems to tell in its favour and ignoring the hundred and one heavy considerations that do not.

Dr Tillyard is more circumspect. He began his study, as he tells us, out of a desire to discover the 'true subject' of *Paradise Lost*. But after all his investigations he certainly does not find himself in a position to tell us in a sentence, as More does,

1 Op. cit. p. 244. 2 Ibid. p. 246.

cautious, looks around till sides

what this true subject is. Indeed, I think it is difficult not to feel some disappointment with Dr Tillyard's concluding summary. He compares the meanings that he considers 'unconscious' with those that are 'conscious', points out certain conflicts and inconsistencies, strikes a kind of balance, and leaves the matter more or less at that. I do not mean to suggest that he ought to have done more: my feeling (indicated in the earlier pages of this essay) is that he ought, if anything, to have done less. It is merely that the high hopes with which we begin his inquiry receive, in the end, no very adequate satisfaction. We do not, after all, find the 'true theme'—only a cluster of reasonably clear intentions interpenetrated by ambiguous half-lights of unrealized motives and dubious under-meanings. It seems to me very likely, on the whole, that the matters that Dr Tillyard finds in *Paradise Lost* and that he calls 'unconscious meanings' really are in the poem. But I think his name for them is wrong. It is a name, I think, that exaggerates their importance, and that to some extent misstates their nature.

What Dr Tillyard finds are half-known feelings: feelings the true quality and strength of which Milton could not admit to himself or else did not understand; these are chiefly what he finds; he finds also a significant change of mood within the poem. These matters have importance, without any doubt. As for feelings, a considerable list of them could be made. It might begin, as Dr Tillyard suggests, with Milton's 'unconscious betrayal of a personal spite against the enticements of women'.[1] It is obvious that numerous other instances of such unconscious betrayal could be given. Dr Tillyard, recognizing this, confines himself to the four chief themes in which, it seems to him, 'unconscious meanings' are to be detected. He heads them: Satan, Christ, Paradise and Pessimism.

It would be hard to quarrel with what Dr Tillyard has to say about Satan. Dr Tillyard is not with the 'Satanists', but

1 Milton, p. 276.

he does not see 'how we can avoid admitting that Milton did partly ally himself with Satan, that unwittingly he was led away by the creature of his own imagination'; and he feels (to my mind, with perfect rightness) that 'it is not enough to say with Saurat that Satan represents a part of Milton's mind, a part of which he disapproved and of which he was quite conscious'.[1] The feeling of most readers would surely be with Dr Tillyard that there is more than conscious recognition, more than conscious disapproval, in all this. The balance *is* disturbed; the poem, instead of being on an even keel, has a pronounced list, and Satan is the cause of it. Dr Tillyard himself makes some attempt to right the balance —to put the poem back on an even keel—by arguing that though Satan stands for 'heroic energy' (something in which Milton devoutly believed and which therefore led him to limn this character with a too strong unconscious sympathy), 'heroic energy' is not absent from the central event of the poem itself. Dr Tillyard, as we have noted, inclines to see in the story of the Fall the meaning that every moment in life is critical—that life is *all* crisis—and in this way, he would suggest, the Fall itself expresses, by negation or in reverse, the 'strenuous Western temper' that Satan in a more positive way brings out. The poem, regarded in this light—with its loading of 'heroic energy' placed not only in the story of Satan but in the story of the Fall as well—recovers, in a sense, its equilibrium. It does not, of course, quite recover it. For even if one grants Dr Tillyard his reading of the Fall, it is still Satan who gives the positive, unmistakable expression to the meaning: the Fall, if it expresses such a meaning at all, can at the most do so by implication and in the weaker, negative way.

But as for the portraiture of Satan: even if we share Dr Tillyard's general view of it, as most of us perhaps do, why should the effect of this portraiture on the poem be

1 Op. cit. p. 277.

termed an 'unconscious meaning'? Satan swings the theme from the straight, makes intense and gripping what should, perhaps, have left us a little less emotionally involved, sets up a tug in the poem not easy to counteract; all this we understand very well; and all this to some extent conflicts with Milton's conscious meaning. But why should the irresistible predilections—the unconquerable interests and bents in Milton's nature—that are behind all this be themselves termed 'meanings'? The term in the context seems confusing, and suggests a parallelism between meanings conscious and meanings unconscious that has, surely, no real existence.

The treatment of Christ presents few difficulties. Milton believed in spiritual regeneration—*really* believed in it—and the story of the incarnate Christ fitted into this belief. The story of the incarnate Christ also happened to be the core of Christianity: Milton therefore could not admit the possibility of disregarding it, even to himself. But Dr Tillyard suggests (and the feelings of most readers, again, must surely chime with his) that Milton would perhaps have been more comfortable if he *had* been able to disregard it, leaving it to man to work out his own salvation. Odd though it sounds, Christianity with the human Christ left out would have suited Milton rather well. To the story of the incarnate Christ, in short, Milton gives a somewhat 'cold, intellectual adherence'. The fact, in *Paradise Lost*, is of no great importance; by this particular 'unawareness' in Milton (unawareness of his own exact feelings) the unity of the poem is not affected.

The third 'unconscious' theme is Paradise, about which Dr Tillyard has two points to make. The first has been noticed indirectly already: it brings what he has to say into touch with Paul Elmer More's theory, which Dr Tillyard would regard as incomplete rather than erroneous. Milton's passionate desire for a golden age is merely a symptom, Dr Tillyard would say, of something deeper in him, this something deeper being the 'enormous energy' of his mind—the same energy that receives its direct expression in the poem in the image of Satan himself. 'Only an active man can create a living picture of sedentary bliss.'[1] And this thought leads the way to a linkage (in my opinion, far too ingenious) of the poignant sweetness of Paradise with Satan and 'energy' and the 'Western temper at its height', and so with the 'main trend' of the poem.

Dr Tillyard's second point seems to me to have more real importance. He observes that it is 'in the daily life of Adam and Eve that Milton's conscious intention breaks down'. In other words, Milton began his poem with the assumption that the unstruggling innocent life of Eden was good— imagining himself really to believe this. But when it comes to the point he has great difficulty in persuading us, and perhaps had a good deal of difficulty in persuading himself, that such a life would not have meant to any human being normally constituted an eternity of boredom. In short, 'he can be no more successful than any other human being in an attempt to imagine a state of existence at variance with the primal requirements of the human mind'.[2] He was mistaken, that is to say, about the exact nature of his material here, about what could be done with it, and about what he himself in his heart of hearts felt concerning it. It is one of those 'paradoxes' of the poem, noted in an earlier chapter. But again, I do not quite see why the term 'meaning' should be employed. Milton's conscious intention breaks down here: that is very evident: but does it break down because of an unconscious intention? Is the breakdown of a conscious intention the equivalent of an unconscious 'meaning'? The word, once more, seems awkward.

The fourth of Dr Tillyard's hidden themes is in some ways the most interesting of all. There is a definite change of mood, he feels, within the poem. The 'pessimism' that seems to him present or latent throughout becomes much more marked

1 Op. cit. p. 284.   2 Ibid. p. 282.

in the last four or five books, and amounts to a change of attitude. It even gets into the texture of the verse, 'causing a less energetic movement'. The restricted scene of these later books may in part—but only in part, Dr Tillyard thinks—be the cause. The true explanation is that Milton himself altered during the writing of the poem. 'The change is very clear. In the first four books, Milton gives energy out; in the last four or five he turns it inwards into himself. In the first it is active; in the last books it has been converted into a stoical resistance.'[1] Buoyancy, expansion, give way to control, contraction; a 'desire to do great deeds' gives way to a desire for inward peace.

There has been much discussion of this alleged change, though it is the sort of matter about which it is easier to convince oneself than anybody else, so much depending on impressions difficult to define and almost beyond proving. Sir Herbert Grierson, in partial qualification of Dr Tillyard's findings, has reminded us that pessimism (the many called, the few chosen) was inherent in the Evangelical Christianity of Milton's age, is inherent indeed in any form of Christianity that is historical; and he suggests that the quiet consoling close should perhaps be allowed to modify somewhat Dr Tillyard's verdict. Dr Tillyard will not have this; he insists that the tone really does change and is as marked as he said. Perhaps it is. It is when we seek to explain it that we must, surely, be cautious. The Restoration came and changed Milton: that no doubt *could* account for changes of mood in the poem: on the other hand it might not be what is really behind them. A dozen causes are possible. Milton, for various reasons, might have become tired; he might have become disheartened; he might have become disillusioned. He might conceivably have become disheartened and disillusioned in some degree about his poem, as well as about England or God. It is merely possible that the final phases

1 Op. cit. p. 291.

of his poem did not interest him quite as intensely as the earlier phases had done, and that for that reason, and for nothing much more profound, some energy went from it. And we must surely be careful, in a case so evasive, affording so little security of hold, how we go about marshalling our evidence. It is well for Dr Tillyard to quote the long speech by Adam near the close (XII, 552–73), with Michael's reply. They do, it is true, appear to sum up impressively what Dr Tillyard calls Milton's 'middle-aged' philosophy of life. It is not so well to take on the opposite side the speech of Beëlzebub (II, 402–9):

> But first whom shall we send
> In search of this new world, whom shall we find
> Sufficient?...

and to quote these lines—so apt and natural, one could almost say so unavoidable, in the circumstances—as signifying the vitality and hopefulness of the earlier Milton. It is curious to note that Dr Tillyard had already advanced Satan's 'anguished impotence' at the beginning as an example of the underlying pessimism of the whole poem.[1] This is blowing hot and cold with a vengeance. Such a method of interpretation is dangerous, surely, in the extreme.

But even if there be, for whatever reason, a genuine change of tone: even if Milton did begin in one mood and end in a mood slightly different: can such a process (which must have many parallels in literature, if we liked to hunt for them) be brought in any reasonable way under the head of an unconscious meaning', or be said to have much bearing on the 'real theme' of the poem?

And I would venture the same suggestion about certain other 'meanings', also 'unconscious', brought forward by Dr Tillyard in his later book, *The Miltonic Setting* (1938). He notes, for example, Milton's power over primitive feeling, how he can reproduce instinctively that awe in the presence

Op. cit. p. 284.

of wild nature that we may imagine formed a powerful element in the consciousness of early man. He gives for one instance the lines from *Comus* ending

On Sands, and Shoars, and desert Wildernesses,

and for another the description by Michael of the Mount of Paradise and how it will be swept by the flood

Down the great River to the op'ning Gulf,
And there take root an Iland salt and bare,
The haunt of Seales and Orcs, and Sea-mews clang. (XI, 829)

Few will deny the powerful effect of such passages, and most of us, no doubt, would like to think that they do in fact depend for their power on ancient memories, mysteriously stirred. Again, when Dr Tillyard speaks of the 'architectonic' quality so pronounced in Milton, the joy he so evidently feels in the triumph and completeness of his shapings, all must acknowledge the rightness of the perception. The examples, once again, that he gives of a feeling in Milton (already noted by M. Saurat) for fertility and exuberant life—'as if his own teeming brain and soaring temperament were in some intimate way linked with the apparent lavishness of nature in perpetuating the forms of life'[1]—must command our prompt assent. Dr Tillyard singles out the phrase 'enormous bliss'; and who indeed could fail to be hit by it, or help feeling something instinctive, something more than artistry or reason, in the perfection of it.

But I still cannot see why Dr Tillyard should object to Professor Grierson that 'he allows for no meaning Milton may be conveying extrinsically to the story or to the theological framework'.[2] Professor Grierson, I expect, has been as powerfully struck by the words 'enormous bliss' as anyone else; but why should he mention Milton's feeling for fertility when he is talking about the theme of *Paradise Lost*? Even Dr Tillyard admits that this feeling, interesting and notable

1 Op. cit. p. 69.   2 Ibid.

though it is, 'has not a great deal to do with the *main* theme of *Paradise Lost*'. It most decidedly has not: and I would suggest that to detach it in any prominence at all as a 'meaning' of the poem is to misuse the word. Let us take a close analogy. Thomas Hardy also had a remarkable sense of the fertility of nature. There are passages in his prose, describing the thrusting energies of spring, that are not unworthy to be compared with Milton's own descriptions of nature's exuberance. One or two passages of the kind occur in *Tess of the D'Urbervilles*. But suppose a critic in discussing the meaning of *Tess* ignored these passages (as it is nearly certain he would), should we feel inclined to complain? Such passages are an enrichment to the book, and possibly in a remote and indirect way they bear on the theme of it—they ought to, if the book is well written. If we must, we could say of them, as Dr Tillyard says of the corresponding passages in *Paradise Lost*, that they convey a 'message', so deep is the recognition they embody. But surely it would be a straining of the processes of criticism to count this seriously as one of the prime 'messages' of *Tess of the D'Urbervilles*. The truth is that this particular 'message', just because it springs from so deep a sense, is likely to announce itself in almost any place in Hardy where the circumstances are at all appropriate.

Dr Tillyard's perception of the 'bounty' in Milton, of Milton's elemental shaping joy, and of the primitive stir in such lines as 'haunt of Seales and Orcs, and Sea-mews clang' (and no critic is richer in such perceptions than Dr Tillyard) connects what he has to say about unconscious meanings with Miss Maud Bodkin's elaborate study, *Archetypal Patterns in Poetry* (1934).

Taking her starting-point in Jung's theory of primordial images—images left obscurely in the mind by countless racial experiences of the same type—she studies the way in which great literature can reawaken such images and so bring very powerful unconscious forces into play, certain poems in this fashion seeming to acquire an emotional significance not explicable purely in terms of any 'meaning' conveyed. She accepts Gilbert Murray's description of the phenomena that she has in mind. Certain stories and situations (the story of Hamlet and the story of Orestes are two instances) seem to be 'deeply implanted in the memory of the race, stamped as it were upon our physical organism'.[1] They are strange to us, yet it is as if we had always known them; when we meet them it is with a mysterious sense of familiarity. Miss Bodkin sets out to explore these ancient themes; they are themes that persist with variation from age to age, and that correspond, as it were, to configurations within the mind itself. These con-figurations are the 'archetypal patterns' that a great poet, without knowing what he is doing, may bring to life once again, re-electrifying, so to say, the old circuits, tapping ancient energies, and so releasing a quantity of emotion that seems quite beyond what the visible, ponderable causes can account for.

The basic conjectures on which Miss Bodkin's thesis rests will be amenable some day, no doubt, to scientific testing. In the meantime no one can read her series of investigations without a new sense of the mysterious powers of literary art, and of the remarkable possibilities of explanation that some day may be brought within our reach. The 'primordial images' that she finds in *Paradise Lost* are those of Heaven and Hell; of Satan as the Devil and as Hero; of God; and of Woman. All these (in her thesis) would involve 'unconscious meanings'; and there is no doubt, whatever the validity of the thesis, that our experience of the poem at these points is enriched by Miss Bodkin's analysis.

Yet it seems clear that such a method, however illuminating, has its dangers. Two of them are relevant, I think, to the present study.

1 Quoted, op. cit. p. 2.

The first—which I may perhaps illustrate most readily by referring to Miss Bodkin's treatment of the *Inferno*—is simplification. Miss Bodkin, in discussing the interrelated images of Heaven and Hell, notes the recurrent symbol of the Cavern and the indefinable fears that appear to cluster round it. May these cavern-feelings, she wonders, be a heritage from the mind of that earlier Europe that conceived the Magdalenian rock-drawings and put them in the lightless depths of those sanctuary caves? It is a question no one can answer; but perhaps poets feel, without knowing what it is they feel, a breath from the ancient ritual. At any rate their sense of the Cavern (with the suggestion in the image of 'archaic depths of the mind itself') seems much the same as this sense always was. Here is an age-old symbol, reviving for us the primitive awe, whether it reaches us through Homer's Tartarus or Virgil's sixth book or Dante's *Inferno* or Coleridge's caverns measureless to man.

Miss Bodkin thus secures a very attractive and persuasive pattern: we appear to have a chain of similar or identical significances.

But let us single out one of these works—the *Inferno*—and think for a moment what it is. Dante and his guide descend into the blind world. Yes: but in a moment or two this world is blind no longer, it has sprung to busy life. When we go over in our minds our true experience of the *Inferno*, is it really possible to feel that Miss Bodkin's cavern-imagery gives any true suggestion of that experience—that it does much more than bring us to the brink of that experience? The *Inferno* with its teeming incident and dramatic wealth, its quality almost of a sinister underground fair: how amid the crowding intensities of such a scene can the basic cavern-imagery exert real pressure on our imaginations? It is almost like asking us to feel truly 'underground' on Piccadilly Circus Station. The living principle of the *Inferno* is human emotion—not caves, or memory of caves. It is surely only in abstraction, when we are away from the poem and not thinking very intensely of what a reading of it *means* from moment to moment, that we can feel the relationship between the *Inferno* and the caverns of *Kubla Khan* to be very real.

Miss Bodkin not only links the *Inferno* with *Kubla Khan* and other 'cave' books: she also plots out a cross-reference to a second archetypal pattern, that of Rebirth. 'The horror of Dante's Hell is made bearable for the reader by the fact that interest is concentrated upon a forward movement. The torments of the damned are described as unending, but they have their effect as incidents in a journey—a transition from darkness to light, from the pangs of death to new life.'[1] The poem from this point of view becomes therefore another example of the Rebirth pattern in literature. The tortures of the damned are said to be eternal; but in a sense we discount this; it is not true to the 'central experience' of the poem. The central experience of the poem is that of a movement from Hell to Heaven, death to birth, dark to light.

This is sympathetic, and yet one wonders whether here again there may not be some tampering with our natural, unforced experience of Dante's work. What would Dante himself have had to say to the suggestion that the eternity of Hell was 'untrue to the central experience' of his poem? We rebel against the notion of the eternal tortures; mercifully, says Miss Bodkin, such a thing does not happen in life as we know it: 'hell', as we know it, is transitional, a phase of suffering, something we are always likely to go into, but may be always sure of coming out of. Dante, unconsciously, was thinking of it in the same way, as the general sweep of his poem shows. It is ingenious; but, again, surely, one does not quite escape the sense of a certain rearrangement of what is given: as if Miss Bodkin, despite her good intentions, were giving slight pats and

1 Op. cit. p. 136.

adjustments to the *Divine Comedy* to make it fit, perhaps a little more exactly than it really does, into the pattern she has in mind. It is, at any rate, a danger inherent in her method.

The second risk is a little harder to define: it amounts, perhaps, only to another kind of simplification.

The presupposition behind Miss Bodkin's whole inquiry is, of course, that we are dealing with good, even great, literature. The primordial images are brought to life again only if the writing is extremely effective: and only if it is *in every way* effective. It is possible, for example, that a poet of unremarkable gifts may at some future date conceive the project of writing still another *Prometheus*; if he should, his success in rousing the ancient pattern of the rebel-hero will depend on one thing: how well he does his work. The name Prometheus is not magical: the story in itself has only a latent virtue, in itself it can guarantee no results. If the archaic images are stimulated it will be because the poet has skill —and great skill. In short, literary power is the condition of all the effects Miss Bodkin studies.

Now when Miss Bodkin discusses the concluding scene of Satan's story—the transformation of the bad angels into serpents and the eating of the ashes—I feel for my own part that what she is saying about the emotional results of this scene has no reality, because this prime condition is not being completely fulfilled. Miss Bodkin takes it for granted, of course, that the scene is in every way effective. That it is in *some* ways effective it would be only stupidity to deny. Miss Sitwell has noted for us her own subtle responses, but anyone at all with an ear for words and rhythms must recognize the triumphs of this passage. Yet (for me at least) its effectiveness in some ways is not compensated for by its ineffectiveness in others. I have tried to argue the matter in a previous chapter, and need not labour the points there made; but as the appeal in such a case—indeed in all the cases that Miss Bodkin discusses—is in the end to individual feeling, I may perhaps offer again, merely as one reader's evidence, my own responses to the passage. I am not, I think, insensitive to what Lascelles Abercrombie saw in it, or to what Miss Sitwell sees in it: I relish its virtuosity and the 'fierce humour' that impregnates it. But I am utterly unable to follow Miss Bodkin when she finds that the 'distinctive music of Milton's verse' and all the other skills that the passage shows—that all these help 'to penetrate our vision of Satan's shame with an element of bitter tragedy'.[1] I feel no tragedy, because I cannot take the passage seriously. I share in few of the emotions that Miss Bodkin apparently feels, because to me the devices of the passage seem as clear as day. Miss Bodkin sums up her general view of Satan: 'In the figure of Satan as hero, we may say, an objective form is given to the self of imaginative aspiration, or to the power-craving, while the overthrow of Satan, and his humiliation as infernal serpent, satisfies the counter movement of feeling toward the surrender of personal claims, and the merging of the ego within a greater power.'[2] I understand the first part of this statement and fully agree with it, for it seems to me to refer to something that really exists in the poem. We are very near, again, to that 'energy' in which Dr Tillyard finds the key to Satan's moving power. But I cannot feel that the second part has any true relation to what actually occurs. The passage delights us by its workmanship and 'satisfies' our nature, no doubt, in various ways. One satisfaction that it brings is the satisfaction, I have suggested, that a comic cartoon supplies. But it is obvious that Miss Bodkin is thinking of satisfactions more elevated than this. The root questions, in such a case, would seem to be, Does the passage provoke in us a full imaginative surrender? Are our feelings genuinely engaged? Miss Bodkin writes: 'When Satan as infernal serpent is surveyed with

1 Op. cit. p. 235.   2 Ibid. p. 244.

fear and loathing, the image of God has the character of strong ally and saviour.'[1] I can only say that to my feeling her 'pattern' here is like something writ in air, a mirage; for me, at least, it is so; for with me the archetype utterly fails to function, so strong is the thwarting effect of my sense of the shallow art and elementary incitements of the scene: of my sense of it, in short, beneath all the rhythmical and verbal wonders, as essentially humbug.

I conclude with a note on still another kind of 'unconscious meaning'. Dr Tillyard, as we have seen, plots the curve in *Paradise Lost* of what he considers to be Milton's increasing pessimism. Professor Arthur Sewell in his book *A Study in Milton's Christian Doctrine* (1939) plots what might almost be described as the counter-curve: the curve of Milton's increasing sense of the goodness of God.

Professor Sewell's view takes in, of course, much more than *Paradise Lost*: his aim is to trace the whole sweep of Milton's spiritual development. He sees a general movement in Milton's mind from hope to faith, from a belief somewhat shallowly grounded in 'the conviction that God had a special mission for England and for himself', to a deeper, humbler, less questioning sense of God as wise and merciful, though inscrutable in his ways. 'During the latter half of the decade 1650–60', says Professor Sewell, 'the wind began to go out of Milton's sails.'[2] His manifold disappointments left him with a view of God 'impoverished and starved of significance,' 'compelling to his mind but chilling to his heart'. To effect a reconciliation between heart and mind was now his task. 'What could be the nature of God—now that Milton could no longer believe in the special care of God for his people? In what relation could Milton, could all men stand with God, now that it seemed no longer possible that God had chosen Milton and England for special work? What were God's

1   Op. cit. p. 246.   2 Op. cit. p. 77.

ways with men?'[1] According to Professor Sewell *Paradise Lost* not only gives Milton's answers to these questions; it also shows him in the very act of finding the answers.

This notion of *Paradise Lost* as not only the record of experience, but also in itself experience, is very appealing; and it is interesting too, to see *Paradise Lost* fitting neatly into the whole curve of Milton's spiritual development, revealing within itself a curve that is exactly continuous with the larger curve. It is interesting to see all this—if one really can. The signs of a spiritual progress within the poem are not as evident to me as they are to Professor Sewell.

Professor Sewell sees the curve in *Paradise Lost* in this way: 'God is at first arbitrary Deity conceived and challenged in the figure of Satan. He becomes more and more—but never perfectly—a Being whose nature is goodness, whose delight it is to communicate his good to those who will receive it. God is not terrible to man, but good. Man is terrible to himself.'[2]

It is true enough, I suppose, that the God of the earlier books of *Paradise Lost* is seen chiefly in the guise of his power: he has to be. There was no escape from that, though the manifestations of the power need not, perhaps, have been made quite so disagreeable. But is it really true to say that this God becomes 'more and more'—even though never

1 Op. cit. p. 78. The expression 'God's ways with men' raises an interesting small point of interpretation. What is the syntax of 'And justifie the wayes of God to men'? Is it 'justifie to men the wayes-of-God', or 'justifie the wayes-of-God-to-men'? It would seem likely that Professor Sewell reads the line the second way. Sir Herbert Grierson, I judge, does the same. Newton also took it that way. The matter could be argued on general grounds, but lines 224–6 in Book VIII seem fairly conclusive:

> Nor less think wee in Heav'n of thee on Earth
> Then of our fellow servant, and inquire
> Gladly into the wayes of God with Man.

The context makes it evident that only one reading is possible here: Raphael looks forward to discussing with Man (Adam) the ways of God; he is returning Adam's compliment. Cf. *Samson Agonistes*, ll. 293–4.
2 Ibid. p. 157.

perfectly—a God of goodness? Professor Sewell is far from demonstrating it. Milton, he says, uses the very word 'goodness' 'in those moments in the poem when there seems to be least of all the veil of reasoning between idea and expression'.[1] Does he? Is there much of a veil between idea and expression in those passages in which Milton exhibits his derisive God? As for the passages in which 'goodness' occurs, and in which we are able to see, according to Professor Sewell, the way Milton's mind was tending, they are scattered at large over the poem and seem to me all eminently natural and normal in their places. Professor Sewell's own quotations come from Books IV, V, VII and XII. (The example from Book V is the morning-prayer of Adam and Eve. It would have been a little odd, after all, if the word 'goodness' had not come into this, and if the praise itself had not been made to sound reasonably heartfelt.) In any case, it would look from this series as if Milton's sense of the goodness of God were at least as marked in the first half of the poem as in the second half. If it were a question of ranging passages of this sort in order, I would make the tentative suggestion myself that no passage in the poem, expressing God's relation to his creatures, has a tenderer ring than the passage in Book X that contains the phrase 'Father of his Familie' (ll. 209–23); and that equal or perhaps next to this in degree of tenderness might come the speech of the Son in Book III (ll. 144–66) that contains the pleading: 'that be from thee farr, That farr be from thee, Father.' On either estimate then—Professor Sewell's or my own—a graph of Milton's developing thought plotted from such passages ought to have the appearance very much of a straight horizontal line.

And if we consider God himself as projected in the poem, the result, it seems to me, should be about the same. Can we detect much real difference? Is there a genuine progress in God? The God who in Book VIII lays up for himself

1 Op. cit. p. 117.

eternal hilarity in the 'quaint opinions wide' of astronomers; who in Book x is still publicly washing his hands of blame; who in Book xi pronounces his sovran will for man in tones as unprepossessing as ever ('let him boast His knowledge of Good lost, and Evil got') and who seems to be thinking of man as an opponent whose feeble moves he has neatly countered and whom now he will proceed to checkmate: is this God profoundly changed? The poem has a certain design and it is obvious that this design required some few protestations of God's 'goodness and paternal love' before the end. God had to be a God of power at the start, and it would have been difficult to let him go without revealing in him some gleams of softer feeling: Milton owed him, and his poem, at least that much. But as for those inward struggles that produced, before the poem was quite finished, the image of a truly kindlier God: they seem to me to be illusion.

CHAPTER VII

CONCLUSION

OCCUPIED as I have been in this survey with 'what happens' in the poem, I have had almost nothing to say about its poetry. Perhaps this is as well, in view of the daunting 'keep off' sign for amateurs that Mr Eliot erected some few years ago. It is true that Mr Lewis since then has gone boldly up to this sign, and, wrenching it out with a few dexterous twists and tugs,[1] has flung it zestfully away. Still, the fact that it was once there—even the sight of the hole it stood in—is enough to cause one amateur, at least, to quake.

In any case the facts of the 'poetry'—or at least of the verse—are much less seriously in question. Critics use different names for what they find; they like it, or they dislike it; they regard it as a calamity, or they regard it as a triumph; but what they find is about the same. When Mr Pound talks of the 'Miltonic rumble' he is referring to what the ears of most of us, for many a long day, have been taught to catch as the majestic rollings and reverberations of Milton's grand style. Whether we call it a grand style or a rumble makes very little difference to what is there.

I do not mean to suggest that all controversies even about the facts of the Miltonic style have been settled. There has been some reconsideration of late, for example, of the epic similes, and an inclination to revise somewhat the traditional view of them. Their use as resting-places for the attention has always been understood. They begin with a real comparison, but then the poet is seduced, so to say, by the charm of his own picture; he continues to dwell on it for no reason at all but that he likes it, and we dwell with him for this extra moment or two of poetic holiday, while the poem

1 Op. cit. pp. 9–11.

pauses; then we return to the main business refreshed. But
the question is asked, Have we sometimes dismissed the
extensions of these similes a little too lightly? Have they
subtler implications, often, and a truer relevance, than we
gave them credit for? Mr Empson has discussed a number
of examples from this point of view.

He examines, for instance, the lines that tell of Satan's
flight up toward the gates of Hell. Satan

> Now shaves with level wing the Deep, then soares
> Up to the fiery concave touring high.
> As when farr off at Sea a Fleet descri'd
> Hangs in the Clouds, by *Æquinoctial* Winds
> Close sailing from *Bengala*, or the Iles
> Of *Ternate* and *Tidore*, whence Merchants bring
> Thir spicie Drugs: they on the trading Flood
> Through the wide *Ethiopian* to the Cape
> Ply stemming nightly toward the Pole. So seem'd
> Farr off the flying Fiend.   (II, 634)

Bentley cut out the whole passage. Pearce, whom Mr Empson
quotes, defended it by pointing out that 'Milton in his
Similitudes (as is the practice of Homer and Virgil too)
after he has shown the common resemblance, often takes
the liberty of wandering into some unresembling Circumstances'. But this, Mr Empson says, would defend equally
well 'an irrelevant piece of description, one which is merely
distracting', and 'one that satisfies the imagination through
implied comparisons relevant to the main impulse of the
poem'. The passage in question seems to him to be 'entirely
of this second sort'. He goes on: 'The ships ply nightly
because Satan was in the darkness visible of Hell; are far off
so that they hang like a mirage and seem flying like Satan
(the word *ply*, sounding like "fly", ekes this out); and are
going towards the Pole, because Satan (from inside) is going
towards the top of the concave wall of Hell. They carry
spices, like those of Paradise, because they stand for paganism
and earthly glory, for all that Milton had retained contact

with after renouncing and could pile up into the appeal of Satan; Satan is like a merchant because Eve is to exchange these goods for her innocence; and like a fleet rather than one ship because of the imaginative wealth of polytheism and the variety of the world.'[1]

I do not quite see how such a matter is to be argued, except by an appeal to the very nature of the epic simile —to the 'feel' of it in the ancient poets and to the 'feel' of it in the scores of examples that Milton himself supplies. It is really Mr Empson who should do the arguing, who should furnish grounds for supposing that what he says from 'They carry spices' to the finish of his comment has the slightest truth. What real reason is there for thinking that Milton had these connections—spices with paganism, Satan's wiles with merchandise, a fleet with polytheism—even dimly in mind? The truth of the matter, surely, is obvious at a glance, and is what it has always been understood to be. Satan at a distance through the murk looks rather like a group of massed sails on the horizon (if it needs Teneriffe or Atlas, in one kind of similitude, to suggest his size and importance it certainly needs a fleet, not a mere ship, to do the same thing in another). Ships on the horizon by an optical illusion often seem to hang in the air. And that is about the end of the comparison. 'Pole' chimes in, in a secondary way; but Mr Empson's later parallels seem to me to be sheer imagination. The odds, at a mild estimate, could surely be put at a thousand to one that Milton never dreamt of them.

Mr Empson takes up a second passage:

> While thus he spake, th' Angelic Squadron bright
> Turnd fierie red, sharpning in mooned hornes
> Thir Phalanx, and begann to hemm him round
> With ported Spears, as thick as when a field
> Of *Ceres* ripe for harvest waving bends
> Her bearded Grove of ears, which way the wind
> Swayes them; the careful Plowman doubting stands

1 Op. cit. p. 171.

> Least on the threshing floore his hopeful sheaves
> Prove chaff. On th' other side *Satan* allarm'd
> Collecting all his might dilated stood,
> Like *Teneriff* or *Atlas* unremov'd.   (IV, 977)

Bentley took objection to the ploughman sentence and cut it out.
Mr Empson comments: 'It certainly makes the angels look
weak. If God the sower is the ploughman, then he is anxious;
another hint that he is not omnipotent. If the labouring
Satan is the ploughman he is only anxious for a moment,
and he is the natural ruler or owner of the good angels.'[1]

Mr Empson's syntax is not always of the simplest, and
I confess that after much study I am still not perfectly
certain whether in this particular instance he is on Bentley's
side or Milton's. But the truth of the matter is again, surely,
as clear as day. The ploughman is neither God nor Satan;
Milton did not dream of identifying him with either; he did
not even think of either in connection with him; the ploughman is simply himself. The sentence, that is to say, neither
helps nor hinders the general comparison, for it has no
connection with it. We have slipped off that comparison.
We are not (or ought not to be) thinking about it—about
God or Satan or the angels or the imminent fight; we have
turned our minds from all those, and for the moment are
thinking only of the ploughman, who looks at his wheat and
wonders how *it* will look on the threshing floor. The simile,
in other words, is quite normal. It is not, perhaps, one of
Milton's best. There is not in the original comparison the
instantaneous flash of rightness that we expect: nothing will
make heavy wind-blown grain a perfectly fit image for a
semicircle of menacing spears: there are too many alien
suggestions.[2] But the ploughman, surely, is the least of the
difficulties. The answer to Bentley's question, 'What are
Sheaves bound up in a Barn to the Phalanx, that hem'd

1 Op. cit. p. 172.
2 Newton compares *Iliad*, II, 147, but the cases are really very different.

Satan?' is: nothing at all. Milton did not for one moment think of the sheaves as forming any part of the analogy, or suspect that his readers would have any such thought. He merely took the liberty, as Pearce admirably expresses it, of 'wandering into some unresembling Circumstances'. The effort to find a continuous relevance in Milton's similes may succeed on occasion, but it is an effort, it seems to me, that can easily overreach itself.

My particular concern has been with *Paradise Lost* as poetic narrative, and when all is said the narrative problems are basic, for the poem is a story or it is nothing. That was the ground Milton chose—an action; those were the coherencies in which he elected to work. We shall go on reading the poem for ever, I presume, for the glory of the writing and for the spirit of Milton that so lives in whatever he wrote. Nevertheless the epic that is *Paradise Lost* stands or falls, as every work of literature ultimately must, by the sense it makes. I do not think that we do it a service, at this time of day, by attempting to inject sense into those parts of it that do not make sense, by attempting to tighten what no ingenuity can ever now make thoroughly firm. Mr Charles Williams re-formed *Paradise Lost* to his own satisfaction: Mr Lewis has re-formed it, along very much the same lines, to his. But I think that they both *have* re-formed it, presenting us with an epic that to some extent screens the real, that to some extent takes its place. It is my conviction that their *Paradise Lost*, in some very important particulars, is not even the *Paradise Lost* that Milton meant. But in any case the *Paradise Lost* that Milton meant is not quite the *Paradise Lost* that Milton wrote, for the *Paradise Lost* that he meant was, in a strict sense, unwritable. We are dealing here with something resembling that effect in physics described by Heisenberg in his 'uncertainty principle'. There are objects in Nature that frustrate every attempt to measure them, for the mere

act of measuring them disturbs them: as soon as they are
approached with a view to measurement they are (in a
sense) no longer there. Milton is in exactly this predicament
with his theme: he cannot embody it, for the very act of
embodiment does something to it that he did not intend.
The truth, quite simply, is that he cannot touch this particular
subject without altering it. We have seen again and again
how this is. Satan turns out to be not quite the Satan Milton
had in mind, and inevitably so. Adam, as Milton conceives
Adam, is an Adam who cannot be presented, for as soon
as the process of presentation begins, distortion occurs; and
the distortion, again, is inevitable, it is of the nature of the
case. Adam cannot speak twenty lines or move an inch
without turning into something different from Milton's conception of him. So, almost exactly, with God. God, as
Milton was able to imagine him, can hardly utter twelve
consecutive lines without antagonizing us. As for the central
situation, it cannot hold. Mr C. M. Bowra says of Adam:
'Like other tragic heroes, he has been faced by a choice
between two conflicting desires, and he follows the wrong
one.'[1] This, I think, is much too easy. I do not think that
in such a comment Mr Bowra is really talking about *Paradise
Lost*. He is talking about a ghost-epic that often in criticism
does duty for *Paradise Lost*: a ghost-epic shaped in our minds
from what we know very well Milton was trying to do.[2] The

1 *From Virgil to Milton* (1945), p. 206.
2 Mr Musgrove, I think, is discussing the selfsame ghost-epic when he
tells us that God is 'wholly good', that Satan is grand only in his native
environment of 'evil', and so on. Such statements have little reference,
surely, to the actual *Paradise Lost*; they float in the void somewhere above
it, among the wraiths of Milton's intentions. Such an attitude would lead
logically, I think, to an abandonment of the very task of criticism. That
Mr Musgrove himself feels a measure of artificiality in it is suggested
by his recommendation that we should go into training, so to speak, for
Paradise Lost by putting in a 'good morning's hate of Satan' before we
trust ourselves among the delusions and the snares, the deceptions and
'false glitters', of the first two books.

test here, I would suggest again, is to imagine how we should have felt if Adam had followed, not the 'wrong' desire, but the 'right' one. Indeed, we do not have to imagine: Miss Harriet Byron has imagined for us and has pointed the truth of the matter once and for all. If we attend, not to the ghost-epic, but to the epic that is there, on the pages, written, we shall feel at once, I think, that Mr Bowra's assessment hardly makes contact with what really occurred in it. In the poem as it is there is a fundamental clash: it is a clash between what the poem asserts, on the one hand, and what it compels us to feel, on the other. That is why we are uneasy, as at something wrong, deep down in the treatment. That is why *Paradise Lost* does not profoundly trouble, profoundly satisfy us, in the manner of great tragedy: it cannot, because of that embedded ambiguity at the heart of it.

I do not think that we wrong Milton or do harm to the poem (which has enough left, in all conscience, to stay it against anything that we can do) by taking stand in this way on what I have called our vantage-point. Mr Hugh Sykes Davies has expressed the opinion that there has been 'a steady and gradual decline in the quality of Miltonic criticism over its whole period', the reason being that 'here, and here only, the classical critics are the best, because they are thoroughly at home in the framework and atmosphere of the classical epic; they liked Milton for the reasons which were important to Milton'.[1] That may be; and perhaps there has been a decline; and perhaps there is still decline. But I cannot discern in the process the inevitability that Mr Sykes Davies seems to see. As critics of Milton we may not be as good as Addison was, but if we are not I suggest that we ought to be ashamed of ourselves. We can never feel Milton's classicism as strongly as Addison could, but I think that with an effort and with study it is possible to feel it well enough; and we have a great many other things to feel that Addison never

1 *The Poets and their Critics: Chaucer to Collins* (1943), p. 90.

dreamt of. In some ways (no credit to us) we are in a better
position for estimating *Paradise Lost* than ever Addison was.
The classical critics 'liked Milton for the reasons which were
important to Milton'. That is plainly true, and it means that
their findings have great value. But it is still left to us to
examine the reasons for which they liked Milton, and for
which Milton expected to be liked, and in the light of our
own literary experience, to reassess them.

I end with a fancy. For narrative the material of *Paradise
Lost* was intractable. Milton did his best with it, but there
were things that he tried to do with it that simply could not
be done. Mr Lewis quotes: *Materia appetit formam ut virum
femina.*[1] It seems to me very doubtful whether the 'materia'
of *Paradise Lost* ever genuinely sought or wanted the 'forma'
of the epic: whether that particular union was ever fore-
ordained. The story of the Fall is *uneasy* within the embrace
of the epic, for this story (to repeat) is not in the full sense
writable at all. To the fancy it seems almost to be seeking
another mode. How one seems to hear, beneath the difficult,
broken sequences of Satan's story a majestic *Symphonie
Satanique*! How readily such a symphony could have absorbed, as an easy transitional passage, the great soliloquy
at the beginning of Book IV that in the narrative, I suggest,
can find (for all its greatness) no plausible or logical warrant.
And, apart from Satan, would it perhaps have been easier,
in such a mode, to bring to life those 'eternal essences' that
Milton seems to be trying to express and that the conditions
of narrative seem again and again to thwart or block? At any
rate we can let our fancy dwell on the unhampered wonders
of such a work, and can imagine them, well enough, from the
wonders of the work that we have. In the finale, we seem
almost to hear the very tones of this phantom-symphony in
the beautiful fadings, echoings, subsidences of the poem: in
all the modulations of that matchless conclusion. The menacing

1 Op. cit. p.

trombones have spoken; then have come the gradual declines, the levellings-off, the anticipations of the end:

> He ended; and thus *Adam* last reply'd...
> To whom thus also th' Angel last repli'd....

Once more, and finally, there is a hint of menace from the trombones, as the two exiles look back to Paradise and see it

> Wav'd over by that flaming Brand, the Gate
> With dreadful Faces throng'd and fierie Armes.

Then the gentler instruments take up with the dying notes and the inimitable close.

STIRLING COUNTY LIBRARY

INDEX OF WRITERS